THE ILLUSTRATED BOOK OF JEWISH KNOWLEDGE

THE ILLUSTRATED BOOK OF JEWISH KNOWLEDGE

by
EDITH and OSCAR TARCOV

Illustrated by
Adam Simone

 FRIENDLY HOUSE PUBLISHERS

Design and art supervision by EZEKIEL SCHLOSS

59-390

Copyright 1959

Friendly House Publishers
Library of Congress catalog card number 59-9972

INTRODUCTION

The words that can lead us to an understanding of the Jewish religion and the history of the Jewish people are many and perhaps beyond counting. For this volume, which is intended for the young student, we have selected about a thousand words. We hope that our selections and the definitions and comments we have written will have practical value for the young person engaged in study; our further and fonder hope is that the knowledge gained from this concisely written book will stimulate the reader to explore the great Jewish books, sacred and secular, past and present, which reveal and make vivid the rich and wondrous life and beliefs of the Jewish people.

While we alone are responsible for whatever errors that may exist in our text, we would express our indebtedness to Rabbi David Mirsky for his helpful suggestions and critical reading of the manuscript, and to Mr. Stan Wexler for his careful checking of our facts.

E.T. and O.T.

to
Miriam, Nathan and Jeannie

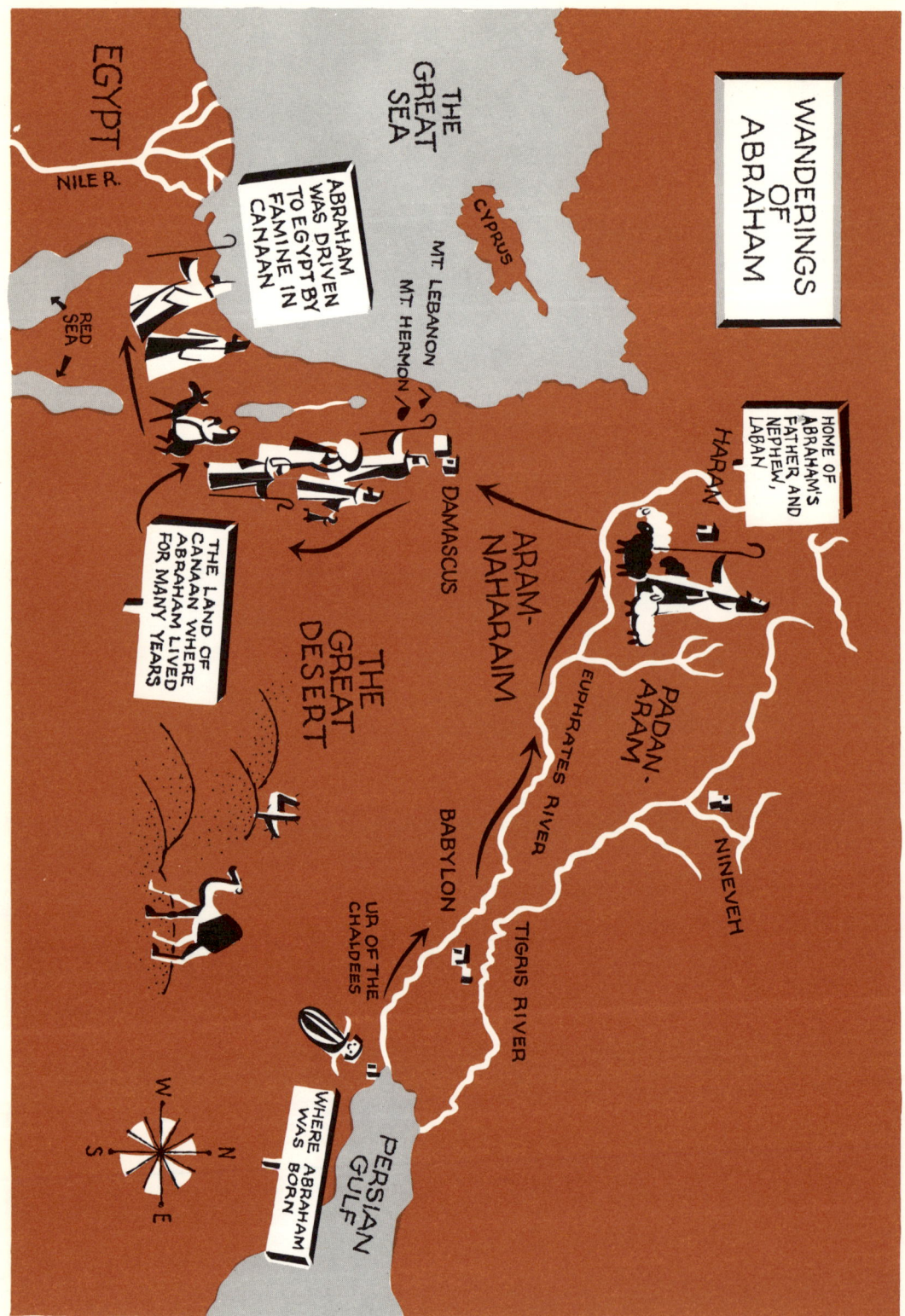

AARON

Elder brother of Moses; ancestor of the Cohanim (*priests*), Moses' spokesman before Pharaoh. After the revelation at Mount Sinai, Aaron was chosen the first high priest of Israel. He was succeeded by his son Eleazar.

ABBA AREKHA

One of the most important Babylonian scholars (about 175-247 C.E.), given the honorary title of Rav *(master, teacher)*, founder of the academy of Sura. He and his colleague and friend, Mar Samuel, helped develop the Babylonian Talmud (Gemara) and established Babylonia as an important center of Jewish life. As a youth Rav studied in Palestine with Judah Hanasi at the time when Hanasi was finishing the Mishnah. Rav made brilliant contributions to the Babylonian Gemara. He composed many prayers, among them the Alenu and the Rosh Hodesh blessings. Abba Arekha is also referred to as Abba the Tall.

ABDON

Of the tribe of Ephraim; one of the Judges of Israel. He judged for eight years.

(Judges, chap. 12:13-15)

ABED-NEGO

see Shadrach

ABEL

Youngest son of Adam and Eve. He was killed by Cain, his angry brother.

(Genesis, chap. 4)

ABIJAH

Also called Abijam, second king of Judah (about 920-917 B.C.E.), son of Rehoboam. Abijah took the territory of Benjamin from the Kingdom of Israel and made it part of the Kingdom of Judah.

(Kings I, chap. 15: 1-8)

ABIJAM

see Abijah

ABIMELECH

Son of Gideon (Jerubbaal) the Judge. He tried unsuccessfully to establish a monarchy when he proclaimed himself king of Israel and selected Shechem as his capital. The tyrannical Abimelech killed 70 of his brothers; only the youngest escaped. He ruled only three years and died ingloriously when, in his siege of Thebez, a millstone shattered his skull.

(Judges, chap. 9)

ABIRAM

see Korah

ABRAHAM

Son of Terah; first of the patriarchs, father of the Jewish people, the first man to believe in the One God and His sovereignty over the whole world. After God made the first covenant with Abraham, he and his wife, Sarah, went to Canaan, the land God had promised him. They had one son, Isaac. Hagar bore Abraham's other son, Ishmael. Abraham, who was born in Ur of the Chaldees, was buried in the Cave of Machpelah.

ABRAM

Name of Abraham before God made His covenant with him.

ABSALOM

Son of King David; famed for his beauty and abundant hair. He tried to overthrow his father, but his revolt failed. He was caught when his hair became entangled in the branches of a tree. Absalom was killed by David's general, Joab, despite David's orders to deal gently with him.

(Samuel II, chap. 14:25-chap. 19:8)

ACADEMIES, BABYLONIAN
The great schools where the Babylonian Talmud was compiled. The three most important were located at Nehardea, Sura and Pumpadita.

ACADEMIES, PALESTINIAN
The great schools in Palestine where the Mishnah was evolved and the Palestinian Talmud was compiled. The most important were located at Javneh, Bet-Shearim, Lydda, Tiberias, Sepphoris, Usha and Caesarea.

ADAM AND EVE
As related in the Book of Genesis, the first man and woman created by God; parents of Cain, Abel and Seth. After eating the forbidden fruit of the tree of knowledge of good and evil, they were driven from the Garden of Eden and were forced to toil for their daily bread.

(Genesis, chaps. 2-3)

ADAR
Sixth month in the Jewish calendar.
see Months, Jewish

ADAR SHENI
The month that is added to the Jewish calendar in leap years. It contains 29 days and is inserted after the month of Adar, before the month of Nisan. It is also called Veadar.

see Months, Jewish

ADDITIONAL SERVICE
see Musaf

ADMAH
One of the Cities of the Plain.
see Cities of the Plain

AFIKOMEN
The piece of matzah hidden during the Passover meal and eaten at its completion. The children, who search for the Afikomen, are rewarded for its return.

AFTERNOON SERVICE
see Minhah

AGGADAH
Aramaic form of the Hebrew word Haggadah (*story* or *narrative*). Aggadah is the part of the Talmud which consists of stories and parables illustrating the meaning of a Biblical passage, in contrast to Halachah which deals with questions of law and religious practice. It was said that, in hard times, "Aggadah refreshes the heart of the people like wine."

see Halachah

AGRIPPA I AND II
see Herodians

AHAB
Seventh king of the northern Kingdom of Israel (about 875-853 B.C.E.), husband of Jezebel, son of Omri. He and Jezebel worshipped the idol Baal. They were cruel rulers who robbed and mistreated the people and persecuted the prophets. The prophet Elijah warned Ahab to return to God but he was not heeded. Ahab died in the battle for the city of Ramoth-gilead.

(Kings I, chap. 16:29-34; chaps. 18-22:40)

AHASUERUS

Powerful king of Persia, husband of Queen Esther. He consented to Haman's evil plot to destroy the Jews of Persia, but Esther succeeded in turning his mind against Haman's plans. Ahasuerus is probably Xerxes who reigned in the 5th century B.C.E. The holiday of Purim celebrates the escape of the Jews of Persia from destruction.

AHAZ

Twelfth king of Judah, son of Jotham and father of Hezekiah, ruled at the time of Isaiah when Assyria destroyed the northern Kingdom of Israel. Under Ahaz' idolatrous rule (about 735-720 B.C.E.), Judah became Assyria's tribute-paying vassal.
(Kings II, chap. 16)

Scholars (Academies, p. 10)

A piece of matzah is hidden (Afikomen, p. 10)

Abraham (p. 9)

Aaron (p. 9)

Ahasuerus (p. 11)

AHAZIAH

1. Eighth king of the northern Kingdom of Israel, ruled from about 853 to 852 B.C.E. The early death of Ahaziah, who was as idolatrous as his father Ahab, was prophesied by Elijah.

(Kings I, chap. 22:52-54; Kings II, chap. 1)

2. Sixth king of Judah, son of Jehoram and Athaliah, grandson of Ahab and Jezebel, worshipper of Baal. While on a visit to his relatives, the idolatrous house of Ahab of Israel, he was slain in Jehu's revolt. Ahaziah ruled from about 843 to 842 B.C.E.

(Kings II, chap. 8:24-chap. 9)

AKDAMUT

A poem recited in the synagogue on Shavuot which extols the greatness of God and the wisdom of Torah.

AKEDAH

(Binding, sacrifice) the Biblical passage recited on Rosh Hashanah which relates the story of God's test of Abraham's faith when he was asked to sacrifice his son and only heir, Isaac.

(Genesis, chap. 22)

AKIBA, BEN JOSEPH

Rabbi, great Tannaitic scholar and teacher (about 50-135 C.E.), helped found the rabbinic tradition. A shepherd of humble birth, he became a scholar with the help of his devoted wife, Rachel. The brilliant views of Akiba and his students were recorded in the Mishnah. Rabbi Akiba supported Bar Kochba's revolt. He died a martyr's death at the hands of the Romans.

ALECHEM HA-SHALOM

Traditional response to the greeting Shalom Alechem. It means "unto you be peace."

see Shalom Alechem

ALEPH BET

The Hebrew alphabet, consists of twenty-two consonants (two of them silent) and five final letters. There are ten vowels in the Hebrew language which are indicated by seven vowel signs.

ALEXANDER JANNEAUS

(Jonathan) Hasmonean king and high priest of Judea (about 103-76 B.C.E.), successor to his brother, Aristobulus I.

ALEXANDER THE GREAT

King of Macedonia, great conqueror, founder of Hellenism, carried Greek culture throughout the ancient world. After he had defeated the Persians at Issus in 333 B.C.E., in his Syrian and Egyptian campaign, he conquered Judea. Jewish history and legend describe him as a friend of the Jews.

ALEXANDRA

see Salome Alexandra

ALIYAH

1. *(Going up)* the term for the honor extended a worshipper who is called up to the reading of the Torah.

2. In modern times the term is also used to describe Jewish immigration to Israel.

ALMEMAR

see Bimah

12

THE HEBREW ALEPH BET

Name	A	B	C	D	E	Sound in Ash-kenazi	Numerical Value	Final Forms
Aleph	א	אִ	אֲ	ﬡ	א	Silent	1	
Bet	בּ	ב	ב	ב	בּ	B	2	
Vet	ב				ב	V		
Gimel	ג	ג	ג	ג	ג	G	3	
Dalet	ד	ד	ד	ד	ד	D	4	
Hay	ה	ה	ה	ה	ה	H	5	
Vav	ו	ו	ו	ו	ו	V	6	
Zayin	ז	ז	ז	ז	ז	Z	7	
Het	ח	ח	ח	ח	ח	CH	8	
Tet	ט	ט	ט	ט	ט	T	9	
Yod	י	י	י	י	י	Y	10	
Khaf	כּ	כ	כ	כ	כ	K	20	ךּ §§
Chaf	כ					CH		
Lamed	ל	ל	ל	ל	ל	L	30	
Mem	מ	מ	מ	מ	מ	M	40	ם §§
Nun	נ	נ	נ	נ	נ	N	50	ן §§
Samekh	ס	ס	ס	ס	ס	S	60	
Ayin	ע	ע	ע	ע	ע	Silent	70	
Pay	פּ	פ	פ	פ	פּ	P	80	ףּ §§
Fay	פ				פ	F		
Tzadi	צ	צ	צ	צ	צ	TZ	90	ץ §§
Kof	ק	ק	ק	ק	ק	K	100	
Resh	ר	ר	ר	ר	ר	R	200	* In Modern Hebrew the ת is sounded as T
Shin	שׁ	ש	ש	ש	שׁ	Sh	300	
Sin	שׂ				שׂ	S		
Tav	תּ	ת	ת	ת	תּ	T	400	
Sav	ת				ת	S*		

A. Ordinary square form characters: Known as כְּתָב אַשּׁוּרִית (Assyrian); this is the most popular form now used for printing Hebrew.

B. Script or cursive form: Used in writing. It is of German origin.

C. Alternate script form

D. Rabbinic form: Used by Talmudic commentators and scholars. It is known as the "Rashi" script. Rashi was the pen name of the renowned French Bible and Talmud commentator (1040-1105).

E. Torah Script: Used for scrolls of the Bible, Mezuzah, Tefillin.

AMALEKITES

Descendants of Esau's grandson Amalek; a warlike, nomadic people who frequently warred against the Israelites. The Amalekites first attacked the Israelites in the desert but they were beaten by Joshua while Moses prayed for victory. Later the Amalekites were again defeated by Saul and David.

(Exodus, chap. 17:8-16; Samuel I, chap. 15:1-9)

AMAZIAH

Ninth king of Judah (796-767 B.C.E.), conquered Edom and captured its capital, Sela. Amaziah warred against Israel and was conquered. He was slain at Lachish and was succeeded by his 16 year-old son, Uzziah.

(Kings II, chap. 14:1-20)

AMEN

(*So be it*) the response upon hearing a blessing or prayer in which the name of God is mentioned.

AMIDAH

Sephardic term for the Eighteen Benedictions (*Shemoneh Esreh*). Amidah means "standing."

see Shemoneh Esreh

AMMONITES

A Semitic people who lived in the land east of the Jordan. Under Joab, the army of David conquered the Ammonites and annexed their land to Israel.

(Samuel II, chap. 10)

AMON

Idolatrous fifteenth king of Judah (about 641-639 B.C.E.), son of Manasseh; father of Josiah. He was murdered after reigning but two years.

(Kings II, chap. 21: 18-26)

AMORAIM

The scholars and teachers whose discussions and interpretations of Mishnah were collected in the Gemara. They were active from approximately the 3rd to the 6th centuries C.E., in Palestine and Babylonia.

AMORITES

A warlike tribe of northern Canaan. They were defeated by Joshua and retreated into the mountains. At the time of King Solomon the Amorites paid tribute to Israel.

AMOS

Third of the Books of the Twelve (Minor) Prophets of the Bible. Amos, a shepherd from Tekoa, lived during the reign of Jeroboam II. He criticized the northern Kingdom of Israel for its frivolity and the great differences between its rich and poor. All men, all nations, Amos insisted, were children of the One God. He warned the Kingdom against the Assyrians and foretold its doom.

AMRAM

Husband of Jochebed, father of Moses, Aaron and Miriam, of the tribe of Levi.

ANGEL

Messenger of God, not necessarily in human form, who conveys God's will to man. The Hebrew word for angel is Malach (*messenger*).

ANOINTING

Rubbing of oil on the head, a religious ceremony that took place when high priests and kings were chosen to assume their new responsibilities. This rite ended with the destruction of the Second Temple. Objects were also anointed, giving them a sacred character.

ANTIGONUS

(Mattathiah) last Hasmonean king of Judea (about 40-37 B.C.E.). He fought unsuccessfully against the supremacy of Herod, the Idumean, whom the Romans appointed king of Judea. At Herod's instigation, the unfortunate Antigonus was executed by the Romans in Antioch, so ending the rule of the Hasmoneans.

ANTIOCHUS IV (EPIPHANES)

The cruel despotic king of Syria. He tried to destroy the Jewish religion and replace it with the Greek gods. He was a cruel ruler to Judea and desecrated the Temple. The Maccabees led the successful revolt against him (165 B.C.E.).

ANTIPAS

see Herodians

ANTIPATER

Governor of Idumea under the last of the Hasmonean kings. Antipater cleverly managed to become governor of all Judea for the Romans. His son, Herod, became king of Judea.

See Herodians

ANTI-SEMITISM

The belief that Jews are an inferior people and should occupy a lower position in society. The lies and the bigotry spread by anti-Semites have been exposed and condemned by the civilized world.

Alexander the Great (p. 12)

The altar of sacrifice (Akedah, p. 12)

Antiochus IV (p. 15)

Akiba, Ben Joseph (p. 12)

Amos (p. 14)

APOCRYPHA

In Hebrew called Ketubim Aharonim (*Other Writings*), books similar to those of the Bible but excluded from it. The Books of the Apocrypha are: I and II Esdras, Tobit, Judith, Additions to Esther, Wisdom of Solomon, Sirach (Ecclesiasticus), Baruch (including the Epistle of Jeremiah), three Additions to Daniel, the Prayer of Manasseh, and I and II Maccabees.

APPLES AND HONEY

Apples dipped in honey are traditionally eaten on Rosh Hashanah as an expression of hope that the coming new year will be sweet and fruitful.

ARAM

1. Grandson of Noah; son of Shem; ancestor of the Aramaeans.
2. Country of the ancient Aramaeans, included Syria and Mesopotamia. The Aramaic city of Damascus was conquered by David but lost by Solomon. Aram, often the enemy of the northern Kingdom of Israel, was invaded by the Israelite kings Ahab and Jeroboam II. It was conquered by Assyria (about 735 B.C.E.) and called henceforth Syria.

see Syria

ARAMAIC

Ancient Semitic language, closely related to Hebrew. Aramaic dialects were spoken by peoples from east of the Jordan to the borders of Assyria and Babylonia. In Babylonian Exile the Jews adopted Aramaic; as a result, parts of the Bible and Talmudic writings and the entire Zohar were written in Aramaic. Aramaic translations of the Bible are called Targum. Many important prayers are said in Aramaic, such as the Kaddish and the Kol Nidre.

ARARAT

The great mountain on which Noah's ark came to rest after the flood. Ararat is a mountain range in Turkey, near Iran.

(Genesis, chap. 8:4)

ARAVAH

(*Willow*) one of the four plants used in the celebration of Sukkot.

(Leviticus, chap. 23:40)

see Sukkot, Four Plants of

see Hoshanot

ARBA KANFOT

(*Four corners*) a rectangular piece of cloth, with an opening for the head and with fringes at each of its four corners; sometimes referred to as Tzitzit. It is worn under a man's regular garments to remind him of God's commandments.

see Fringes

ARBA TURIM

see Turim

ARBOR DAY

see Hamishah Asar Bishvat

ARCHELAUS

see Herodians

ARISTOBULUS I

(Judah) Hasmonean king and high priest of Judea (about 104-103 B.C.E.), son and successor of John Hyrcanus. Aristobulus was the first Hasmonean who assumed the title of king.

ARISTOBULUS II

Hasmonean prince who seized the throne (about 67 B.C.E.) and the high priesthood from his brother, Hyrcanus II. Pompey, the Roman, dethroned Aristobulus and sent him to Rome as a captive.

ARK OF THE COVENANT

Built by Moses at God's command to house the Tablets of the Law; constructed by the artisan Bezalel. It was placed in the Holy of Holies of the Tabernacle in the wilderness. After the Israelites settled in Canaan, the Ark was taken to the sanctuary at Shiloh. At the time of Eli it was captured by the Philistines who later abandoned it. For a century it was guarded by faithful priests at Kiriath-jearim, until King David brought it to Jerusalem. Later it was deposited in Solomon's Temple. The eventual fate of the Ark is unknown.

(Samuel I, chaps. 4-7; Samuel II, chap 6; Kings I, chap. 8)

ARON HAB'RIT

Hebrew name for Ark of the Covenant.

ARON HAKODESH

The holy ark which houses the Torah. Because it encloses the most precious spiritual possession of the Jew, the ark is considered holy. It is often the most beautifully decorated part of the synagogue.

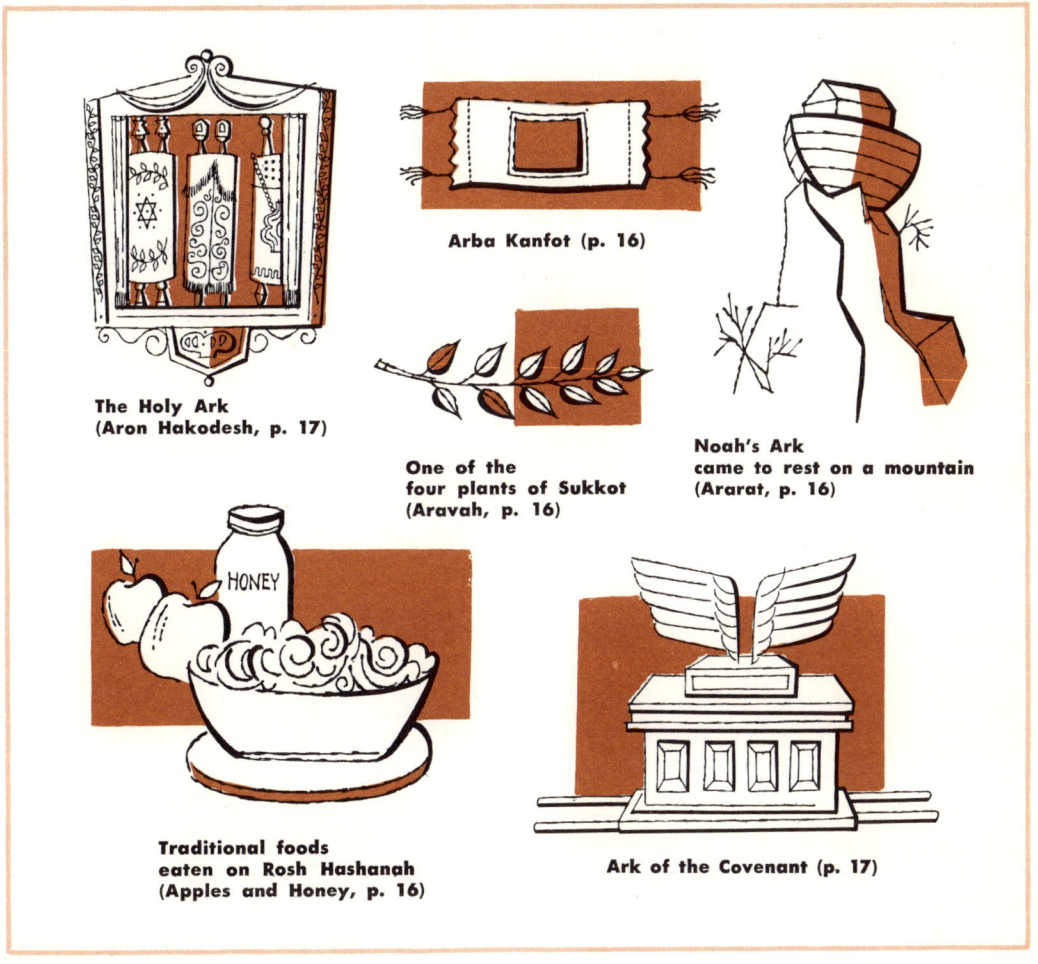

The Holy Ark
(Aron Hakodesh, p. 17)

Arba Kanfot (p. 16)

One of the
four plants of Sukkot
(Aravah, p. 16)

Noah's Ark
came to rest on a mountain
(Ararat, p. 16)

Traditional foods
eaten on Rosh Hashanah
(Apples and Honey, p. 16)

Ark of the Covenant (p. 17)

ARTAXERXES I

King of Persia, about 465-425 B.C.E. He was sympathetic and helpful to the Jews returning to their homeland from Babylonian Exile. He appointed Nehemiah, his cup-bearer, governor of Judea and granted money for the rebuilding of the Temple.

(Nehemiah, chaps. 1-2:10)

ASA

Third king of Judah (about 917-876 B.C.E.), son of Abijah. Asa rid Judah of idol worship and upheld the religion of the One God.

(Kings I, chap. 15: 9-24)

ASARAH BETEVET

(*The Fast of the Tenth of Tevet*) a fast day commemorating the beginning of the siege against Jerusalem by the Babylonians in 586 B.C.E.

ASENATH

Egyptian wife of Joseph, mother of Ephraim and Manasseh.

(Genesis, chap. 41:45)

ASHDOD

see Philistines

ASHER

Eighth son of Jacob; second son of Zilpah, ancestor of the tribe of Asher.

ASHER, TRIBE OF

One of the Israelite tribes. Its territory extended from Mount Carmel and the lower Kishon plain to the Phoenician plain. The tribe conducted a profitable trade with the Phoenicians. Asher eventually became part of the Kingdom of Israel. Asher's banner was pearl; its emblem was a woman and an olive tree. The stone representing the tribe of Asher in the high priest's breastplate was probably a beryl.

ASHI

Outstanding Babylonian scholar (about 354-427 C.E.), noted collector, codifier and editor of the Babylonian Talmud, with his brilliant assistant and successor, Rabina. Ashi, of a wealthy and scholarly family, was beloved for his purity, charity and learning. He was called Rabbana, a title usually bestowed upon the Exilarchs.

ASHKENAZIM

Originally Jews from Germany (and France), as distinguished from Sephardim (Jews from Spain and Portugal). During the times of medieval oppressions, Ashkenazim migrated to the eastern countries of Europe, and later to other parts of the world. Today Ashkenazim no longer primarily refers to a geographical division of Jewry. Ashkenazic rituals and pronunciation of Hebrew differ somewhat from the Sephardic. The majority of Jews are Ashkenazim.

ASHKELON

see Philistines

ASSYRIA

Ancient empire of mighty warriors, artists and builders. From its capital Nineveh, on the upper Tigris, Assyria ruled the Middle East (about 2000-600 B.C.E.). It made Judah a vassal state and destroyed Israel (about 722 B.C.E.). The Assyrians were eventually overrun and defeated by the Babylonians (Chaldeans).

THE ASSYRIAN EMPIRE AT THE TIME OF THE DESTRUCTION OF THE KINGDOM OF ISRAEL

ATHALIAH

Queen of Judah (about 842-836 B.C.E.), daughter of Ahab and Jezebel, wife of King Jehoram of Judah. After the death of her son, King Ahaziah, she seized the throne and had the entire house of Jehoram killed. Prince Joash, an infant, alone escaped her—he was saved by the wife of the priest Jehoiada who later headed the revolt against Athaliah that led to her death. She was the seventh ruler of Judah.

(Kings II, chap. 11)

AV

Eleventh month in the Jewish calendar.
see Months, Jewish

AV BET DIN

(*Father of the court*) one of the two presiding officials of the Great Sanhedrin.
see Zugot

AZARIAH

see Uzziah

BAAL

Idol, often represented as half steer, half human, worshipped by the ancient Canaanites and Phoenicians. Elijah and other prophets warned the Israelites against the worship of Baal. Baal means "lord, master."

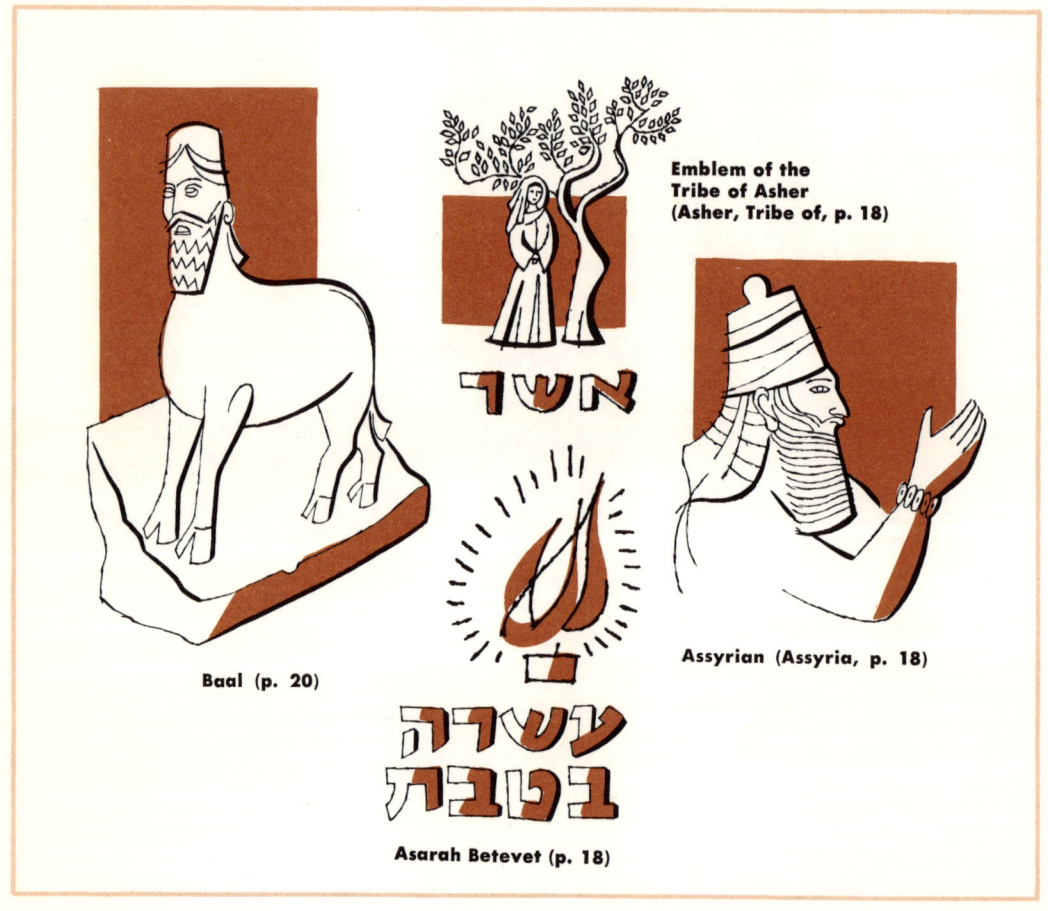

Baal (p. 20)

Emblem of the Tribe of Asher (Asher, Tribe of, p. 18)

Assyrian (Assyria, p. 18)

Asarah Betevet (p. 18)

BAAL KORE

(*Master-reader*) the man who reads and chants from the Torah. In some synagogues he is a paid functionary.

BAAL MAFTIR

see Maftir

BAAL SHEM TOV

Also called Baal Shem (*master of the good [divine] name, he who wrought miracles*), born Israel Ben Eliezer (1699-1760) in the Ukraine, founder of Hasidism, saintly rabbi and great mystic scholar and teacher. The Baal Shem's life and deeds have given rise to many Hasidic legends. The Bal Shem gave new religious strength and joy to the disheartened Jews of Eastern Europe. His ideas have influenced modern religious thought.

BAAL TOKEA

(*Master-Blower*) an expert in the blowing of the Shofar on Rosh Hashanah and Yom Kippur.

BAASA

Third king of the northern Kingdom of Israel (about 914-890 B.C.E.). He was also called Baasha.

BABYLON

Ancient capital of Babylonia on the banks of the Tigris, dates back to the 4th millennium B.C.E. Babylon was noted for its excellent fortifications, well-planned structure and great beauty. In Babylon, under King Nebuchadnezzar, about 586 B.C.E., Jews experienced their first exile. Parts of this ancient city have been excavated by modern archeologists.

BABYLONIA

One of the great empires of antiquity, dates back to before the reign of King Hammurabi in the 20th century B.C.E. One of the later Babylonian (Chaldean) kings, Nebuchadnezzar, led the Jews into captivity to Babylon (586 B.C.E.). When the Persians conquered Babylonia, the Jews were allowed to return to their own land (538). After the destruction of the Second Temple (70 C.E.) and until the 11th century, it was a great center of Jewish life and learning.

(Kings II, chaps. 24-25; Ezra, chap. 1)

BABYLONIAN ACADEMIES

see Academies, Babylonian

BABYLONIAN EXILE

see Exile, Babylonian

BABYLONIAN TALMUD

see Talmud, Babylonian

BALAAM

Soothsayer asked by King Balak of Moab to curse the Israelites whom he feared. On his way, Balaam's ass spoke to him and reminded him of the will of God. Balaam blessed the Israelites instead of cursing them.

(Numbers, chaps. 22-24)

BALAK

Moabite king who sought to destroy the Israelites when they were passing around Moab, on their way to Canaan, by asking Balaam, the soothsayer, to curse them.

(Numbers, chap. 22)

BAMIDBAR

see Numbers, Book of

BARAK

The general whom Deborah inspired to a great victory over the Canaanite King Jabin, and his general, Sisera, near Mount Tabor. His victory is described in the Song of Deborah.

(Judges, chaps. 4-5)

BAR KOCHBA

(*Son of a star*) leader of the ill-fated Jewish revolt against Rome (132-135 C.E.). His enthusiastic followers, included Rabbi Akiba, who, according to the Talmud, changed his name from Bar Kozeba to Bar Kochba, believing him to be the Messiah. At first his army retook many Judean towns, but later it was systematically defeated by Severus, Emperor Hadrian's general. The revolt ended with the fall of the fortress Betar. Many legends are told about Bar Kochba.

BAR MITZVAH

(*Son of the Commandment*). A boy becomes Bar Mitzvah at the age of 13. On the Sabbath closest to his thirteenth birthday he is called up to the Bimah in the synagogue to read from the Torah, usually its concluding portion *(Maftir)*, and from the Haftarah. The ceremony signifies that he has become of age to assume full religious responsibilities as a Jew.

BARUCH, BOOK OF

Book of the Apocrypha, contains sermons, prayers and prophecies of Baruch, disciple of Jeremiah.

Baal Tokea (p. 21)

Reading from the Torah (Baal Kore, p. 21)

Bar Kochba (p. 22)

Bar Mitzvah (p. 22)

Baal Shem Tov (p. 21)

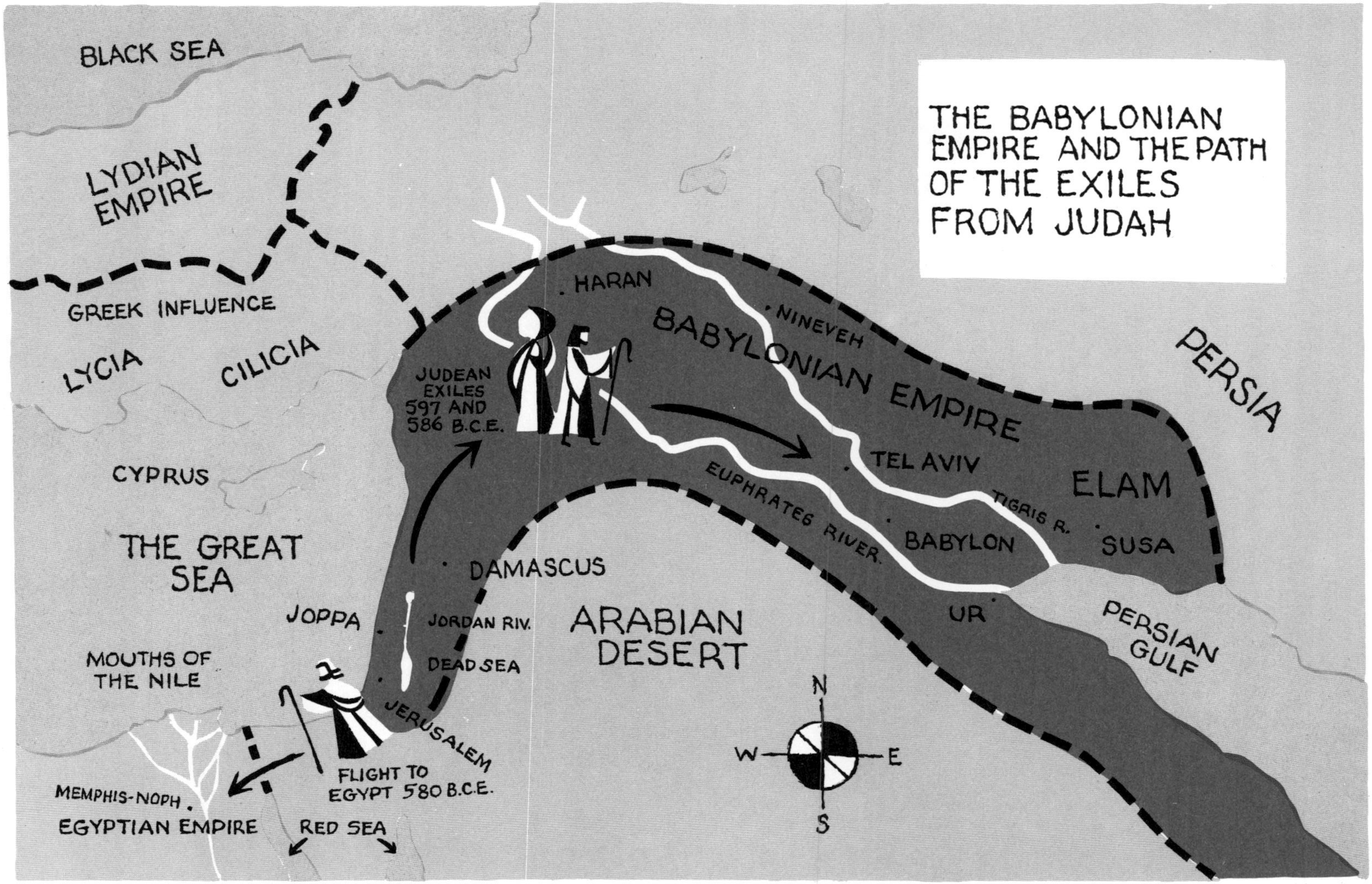
THE BABYLONIAN EMPIRE AND THE PATH OF THE EXILES FROM JUDAH
BLACK SEA
LYDIAN EMPIRE
GREEK INFLUENCE
LYCIA
CILICIA
CYPRUS
THE GREAT SEA
JOPPA
MOUTHS OF THE NILE
MEMPHIS-NOPH
EGYPTIAN EMPIRE
RED SEA
FLIGHT TO EGYPT 580 B.C.E.
JERUSALEM
DEAD SEA
JORDAN RIV.
DAMASCUS
JUDEAN EXILES 597 AND 586 B.C.E.
HARAN
NINEVEH
BABYLONIAN EMPIRE
TEL AVIV
EUPHRATES RIVER
BABYLON
TIGRIS R.
UR
ELAM
SUSA
PERSIA
PERSIAN GULF
ARABIAN DESERT
N
S
E
W

BARUCH HASHEM

(*Blessed be His Name; thank God*). Many Jews say this in response to the question, "How are you?" and when reporting happy news.

BATH-SHEBA

Favorite wife of King David, the widow of the warrior Uriah. She was the mother of King Solomon.

(Samuel II, chaps. 11-12)

BAT MITZVAH

(*Daughter of the Commandment*) the ceremony observed by Reform and Conservative congregations that celebrates the entrance of a Jewish girl into religious life. It is of recent origin. In some synagogues the Bat Mitzvah is called to the Bimah to the reading of the Torah.

BECHOR

First-born son.

see Pidyon Haben

BEDIKAT HAMETZ

(*The searching for leaven*) a symbolic ceremony that takes place the night before the eve of Passover. After all leaven is removed from the home, pieces of bread are placed about the house, and then searched for and collected with the aid of a wooden spoon, a candle and a feather.

BEER-SHEBA

A holy city in southern Israel that had seven wells, a grazing area and watering place used by all the Patriarchs. It was the southernmost city of Israel (hence the well-known expression, "From Dan to Beer-sheba").

BELSHAZZAR

Last king of Babylonia. Daniel interpreted for him the famous "writing on the wall," the Mene Tekel, which predicted the terrible end of his kingdom.

(Daniel, chap. 5)

BENJAMIN

Twelfth and youngest son of Jacob; son of Rachel, only full brother of Joseph. He was the ancestor of the tribe of Benjamin.

BENJAMIN, TRIBE OF

One of the Israelite tribes. Its territory, in central Canaan, between Judah and Ephraim, included Jericho, Ramah, Bethel, Kiriath-jearim and, on its border, Jerusalem (after David's conquest of the Jebusite fortress). Benjamin became part of the southern Kingdom of Judah. Benjamin and Judah are the two surviving tribes. Benjamin's banner was of many colors: its emblem was a wolf. The stone representing Benjamin in the breastplate of the high priest was probably a jasper.

BERESHIT

see Genesis

BESAMIM BOX

see Spicebox

BETAR

see Bar Kochba

BET DIN

(*Court of justice*) in ancient times a court that had the power to decide on matters of criminal and civil law. In the United States the Bet Din makes decisions only on religious matters, and acts as a court of arbitration.

BET HAKENESET

(*House of Assembly*) one of several terms for a synagogue.

BET HAMIDRASH

(*House of Study*) a building for study and prayer for members of the community. In modern times, the Bet Hamidrash usually adjoins the synagogue. It is often equipped with a library and other facilities for study. Prayer is also held in the Bet Hamidrash.

BET HATEFILAH

(*House of Prayer*) another term for a synagogue.

BET HAMIKDASH

(*The Holy Temple*) refers to the First and Second Temples in Jerusalem.

see Temple, First and Second.

BETH-EL

(*House of God*) ancient place of worship, town between Jerusalem and Shechem where Abraham and Jacob built altars. Jacob erected an altar in commemoration of the famous dream he had there.

(Genesis, chap. 28:10-22)

BETHLEHEM

(*House of Bread*) town in a fertile district of Judea, near Jerusalem. Bethlehem was the home of the family of David—Boaz, Ruth and Jesse—and David's birthplace. Rachel's grave is near Bethlehem.

BET-SHEARIM

City in Galilee, seat of Jewish learning at the time of the Tannaim (2nd century C.E.). The Sanhedrin, under Judah Hanasi, met there for a period of time.

see Javneh, Academy of

BEZALEL

Gifted, wise and pious artist and builder of the Tabernacle and the Ark of the Covenant, appointed to this holy task by God through Moses. Bezalel also fashioned all the vessels

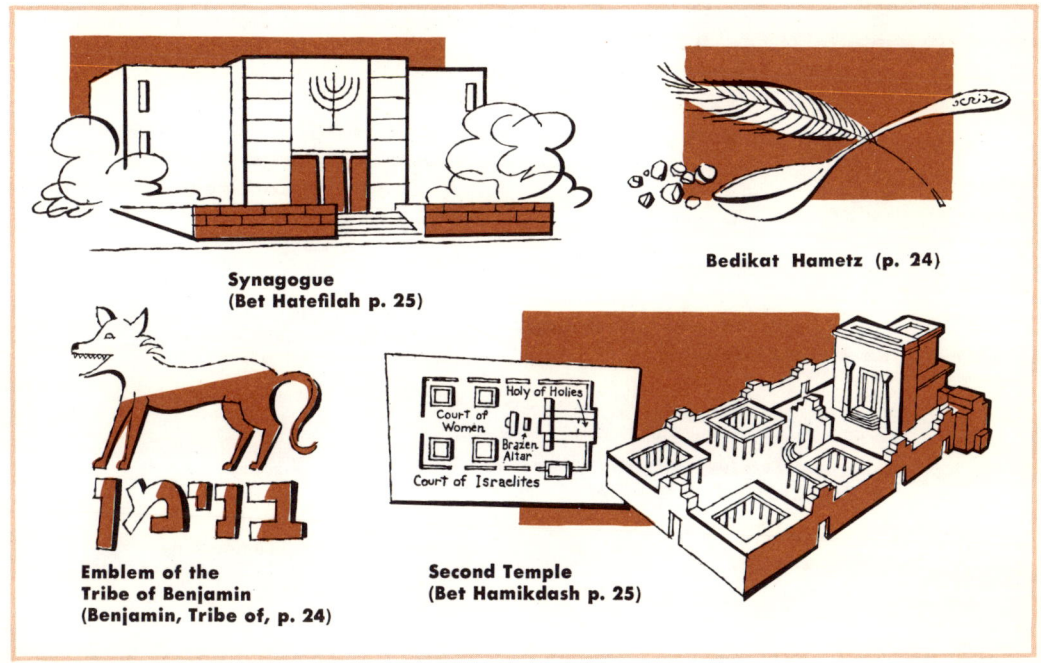

Synagogue
(Bet Hatefilah p. 25)

Bedikat Hametz (p. 24)

Emblem of the
Tribe of Benjamin
(Benjamin, Tribe of, p. 24)

Second Temple
(Bet Hamikdash p. 25)

and instruments of the sanctuary, including the high priest's Ephod and his breastplate with the Urim and Tummim. Bezalel was aided by Oholiab.

(Exodus, chap. 31:1-11; chap. 35:30—chap. 39)

BEZER
City of Refuge, in the territory of the tribe of Reuben.

see Cities of Refuge

BIBLE
From the Greek word Biblia *(books)*, the collected sacred books. In Hebrew called Tanakh, it consists of 24 books (or 39, if the sub-divisions are counted separately). The Bible is also called the Holy Scriptures.

BIBLE, BOOKS OF THE
see Tanakh

BILHAH
Maid of Rachel; secondary wife of Jacob, mother of Dan and Naphtali.
(Genesis, chap 30: 1-8)

BIMAH
The elevated platform in the synagogue, also called Almemar. From a desk on the platform, the Torah and Haftarah are read on the Sabbath and holidays.

BIRKAT COHANIM
The Priestly Blessing of the congregation that was given daily by the priests *(Cohanim)* of the Temple. Today it is part of the synagogue service during morning prayers and during Musaf on holidays, especially on Yom Kippur. The Birkat Cohanim is

BOOKS OF THE BIBLE — THE TANAKH

I. THE PENTATEUCH — THE TORAH
The Five Books of Moses
1. Genesis — Bereshit
2. Exodus — Shemot
3. Leviticus — Vayikra
4. Numbers — Bamidbar
5. Deuteronomy — Devarim

II. THE PROPHETS — NEVI'IM
a. Early Prophets — Nevi'im Rishonim
1. Joshua — Yehoshua
2. Judges — Shofetim
3. Samuel, I — Shemuel, Aleph
   Samuel, II — Shemuel, Bet
4. Kings, I — Melakhim, Aleph
   Kings, II — Melakhim, Bet

b. Later Prophets — Nevi'im Aharonim
The Three Major Prophets:
Isaiah — Yeshayah
Jeremiah — Yirmeyah
Ezekiel — Yehezkeel

The Twelve (Minor) Prophets — Tre Nevi'im
Hosea — Hoshea
Joel — Yoel
Amos — Amos
Obadiah — Ovadyah
Jonah — Yonah
Micah — Mikha
Nahum — Nahum
Habakkuk — Habakkuk
Zephaniah — Zephanyah
Haggai — Haggai
Zechariah — Zekhariah
Malachi — Malakhi

III. THE HAGIOGRAPHA — KETUBIM
(Sacred Writings)
a. The Three Poetical Books — Sifre Emet (Books of Truth)
Psalms — Tehillim
Proverbs — Mishle
Job — Iyob

b. The Five Scrolls — The Megillot
Song of Songs — Shir Hashirim
Ruth — Rut
Lamentations — Ekhah
Ecclesiastes — Kohelet
Esther — Esther

c. The Historical Books
Daniel — Daniel
Ezra — Ezra
Nehemiah — Nehemyah
Chronicles, I — Divre Hayamim, Aleph
Chronicles, II — Divre Hayamim, Bet

said over the congregation with raised hands either by the cantor, rabbi or by a group of Cohanim. In some congregations it is customary for the rabbi or cantor to end the service with this prayer as a closing benediction.

(Numbers, chap. 6:22-27)

BIRKAT HAMAZON
see Grace After Meals

BIUR HAMETZ
The traditional "burning of the leaven." On the morning preceding the first Seder on Passover Eve, the last leaven remaining in the house is burned.

BOAZ
Wealthy farmer of Bethlehem. He helped Ruth when she was a stranger who gleaned the grain from his field, and later married her. They were ancestors of King David.

BREASTPLATE
1. (*Hoshen Mishpat* — Breastplate of Judgment) specifically the high priest's breastplate worn over his robe and attached to the Ephod. It was a finely made square shield of gold on which were set twelve precious stones in four rows (*Turim*). Each tribe of Israel was represented by its own stone engraved with its name. Under the breastplate were, some believe, the Urim and Tummim, two small sacred objects, possibly lots. The high priest wore the Breastplate of Judgment over his heart when he stood before God in prayer and in search for advice and judgment, especially on the High Holy Days.

(Exodus, chaps. 28 and 39)

2. (*Tas*—plate) decorative shield suspended by silver chains over the Torah, resembling the breastplate worn by the high priests.

B'RIT
(*Covenant*) the holy bond God made with Abraham and that He renewed through Moses with the whole people of Israel by giving the Tables of the Covenant (*Luchot HaB'rit*) on which were written the Ten Commandments.

see Covenant

(Genesis, chap. 15; chap. 17: 1-14)

B'RIT MILAH
The rite of circumcision performed when a boy is eight days old. The ceremony signifies the parents' agreement to raise their son as a member of the Jewish community.

see Covenant

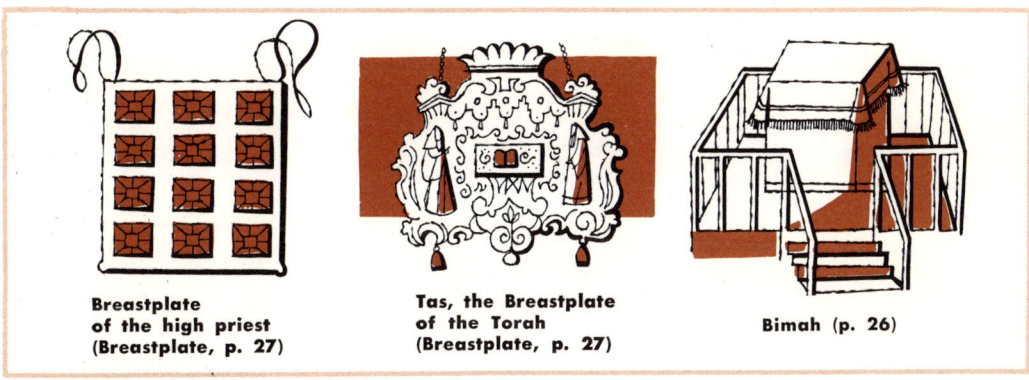

Breastplate of the high priest (Breastplate, p. 27)

Tas, the Breastplate of the Torah (Breastplate, p. 27)

Bimah (p. 26)

CABALA

The tradition of Jewish mysticism. The Zohar is the basic book of Cabala. Cabalistic ideas on the hidden meanings in the Torah were never widely accepted, but they had an influence on Jewish thought. The Hasidim, for example, based many of their beliefs on the teachings of the Cabala.

CAESAREA

Port city on the Mediterranean built by Herod. It was a center of Jewish revolt against Rome during the time of Bar Kochba. Rabbi Akiba and other martyrs were executed there. In the 3rd and 4th centuries, a Talmudic academy flourished in Caesarea, whose Amoraim made great contributions to the Palestinian Talmud.

CAIN

Son of Adam and Eve. He killed his younger brother Abel in a fit of anger. Thereafter he was a restless fugitive and vagabond, and his forehead bore the "mark of Cain."

(Genesis, chap. 4)

CALEB

One of the 12 scouts sent with Joshua to survey Canaan. He and Joshua encouraged the people with reports that Israel was strong enough to occupy it. Joshua and Caleb were the only Israelites who left Egypt and survived to settle in the Holy Land.

(Numbers, chaps 13-14)

CALENDAR, JEWISH

Consists of 12 months in ordinary years and 13 months in leap years, based on the revolutions of the moon, the lunar system (the secular calendar is based on the solar system). Leap years occur 7 times in every 19 years. The numbering of the years is based on the calculation that the Creation took place in 3761 B.C.E. The calendar took its present form in the 13th century and was based on the formulations made by Hillel II in the 4th century.

see Months, Jewish

CANAAN

Early name for the land of Israel; the territory between the Jordan and the Mediterranean, also called the Promised Land, the Holy Land and Palestine.

CANAANITES

The inhabitants of Canaan. They were conquered by the invading Israelites under Joshua. At the time of the Judges, Deborah and Barak defeated the Canaanites in the battle at Mount Tabor, when the Canaanites' mighty iron chariots were stuck in the mud of the swelling River Kishon.

CANTOR

(Hazan) in modern times the official of the synagogue who assists the rabbi in leading the congregation in prayer. He sings many of the prayers and often possesses considerable musical ability.

CARMEL, MOUNT

The beautiful mountain on the Mediterranean whose eastern ridge is watered by the River Kishon. At Mount Carmel, Elijah defeated the prophets of Baal.

(Kings I, chap. 18)

CARO, JOSEPH

see Shulhan Arukh

CAVE OF MACHPELAH

see Machpelah

JEWISH CALENDAR

f Fast day

TISHRI (September-October)
- 1 Rosh Hashanah
- 2 Rosh Hashanah, Second Day
- 1–10 The Ten Days of Penitence
- 3 Tzom Gedaliah f
- 10 Yom Kippur f
- 15 Sukkot (9 days—15th-23rd)
- 16 Sukkot, Second Day
- 17-21 Hol Hamoed of Sukkot
- 21 Hoshanah Rabbah
- 22 Shemini Atzeret
- 23 Simhat Torah

HESHVAN (October-November)

KISLEV (November-December)
- 25 Hanukkah (8 days—25th of Kislev—2nd of Tevet)

TEVET (December-January)
- 2 Last Day of Hanukkah
- 10 Asarah Betevet f

SHEVAT (January-February)
- 15 Hamishah Asar Bishvat

ADAR (February-March)
- 13 Taanit Esther f
- 14 Purim
- 15 Shushan Purim

VEADAR added in leap years (March-April)
- 13 Taanit Esther f
- 14 Purim
- 15 Shushan Purim

NISAN (March-April)
- 14 Taanit Behorim f
- 15 Passover (8 days—15th-22nd)
- 16 Passover, Second Day 1st of the 50 days of Omer (or Sefirah)
- 17-20 Hol Hamoed of Passover
- 21 Passover, Seventh Day
- 22 Passover, Eighth Day

IYAR (April-May)
- 18 Lag B'omer 33rd day of Omer

SIVAN (May-June)
- 6 Shavuot, First Day End of the 50 days of Omer (Sefirah)
- 7 Shavuot, Second Day

TAMMUZ (June-July)
- 17 Shivah Asar Betammuz f

AV (July-August)
- 9 Tishah B'av f

ELUL (August-September)

ASTROLOGICAL SYMBOLS FOR THE JEWISH MONTHS

Tishri — Heshvan — Kislev — Tevet — Shevat — Adar
Nisan — Iyar — Sivan — Tammuz — Av — Elul

CHALDEANS

People of Chaldea in southern Babylonia at the time of Abraham; the land between the Tigris and Euphrates. The latter Babylonians were also called the Chaldeans. They, with the help of the Medes, overthrew Assyria (about 612 B.C.E.). The Babylonian king, Nebuchadnezzar, was a Chaldean. Abraham was born in Ur of the Chaldees.

CHARITY

see Zedakah

CHOIR

The use of choirs at religious services dates back to the time when the Levites sang in the First Temple. Later, there were periods of opposition to their use in the synagogue. Today many synagogues have well-trained choirs.

CHRONICLES, I AND II

(*Divre Hayamim*) the last two books of historical writings in the 3rd division (*Ketubim*) of the Bible. Chronicles retell the history of Israel from the time of Saul to the return of the Jews to Judea from Babylonian Exile.

CIRCUMCISION

see B'rit Milah

CITIES OF REFUGE

Six sacred cities of refuge for men who had unintentionally killed. No refuge from prosecution, however, was extended to a willful murderer. These cities—Bezer, Ramoth-gilead, Golan, Kedesh, Shechem and Hebron —existed as refuges until the destruction of the Second Temple.

(Numbers, chap. 35; Deut., chap. 4:41-43; Joshua, chap. 20)

CITIES OF THE PLAIN

The cities of Sodom, Gomorrah, Admah, Zeboiim and Zoar. These wicked, inhospitable cities, in the fruitful valley of the Jordan, with the exception of Zoar, were destroyed by fire and brimstone. Their ruins lie on the bottom of the Dead Sea. Zoar was saved for Lot's sake.

(Genesis, chap. 14: 1-3; chap. 18:16-chap. 19:29)

CITRON

see Ethrog

CITY OF DAVID

see David, City of

CODES OF JEWISH LAW

Systematic explanations of the laws governing Judaism. The Torah is the foundation of all Jewish law upon which all later codes are based. The Talmud, the greatest post-Biblical collection of Jewish law, elaborates and explains the laws of the Torah. The most famous post-Talmudic codes are: Maimonides' Mishneh Torah (12th century), Jacob Ben Asher's Turim (14th century), Joseph Caro's Shulhan Arukh and its Ashkenazic addition, Moses Isserles' Mappah (both 16th century).

COHANIM

(Singular, Cohen) the priests in Israel, descendants of Aaron. Today Cohanim still receive special honors in the synagogue service. They receive the first Aliyah and give the priestly blessing *(Birkat Cohanim)*. In the ancient Temple, only the Cohanim could perform the most sacred tasks and rituals.

COMMANDMENT

see Mitzvah

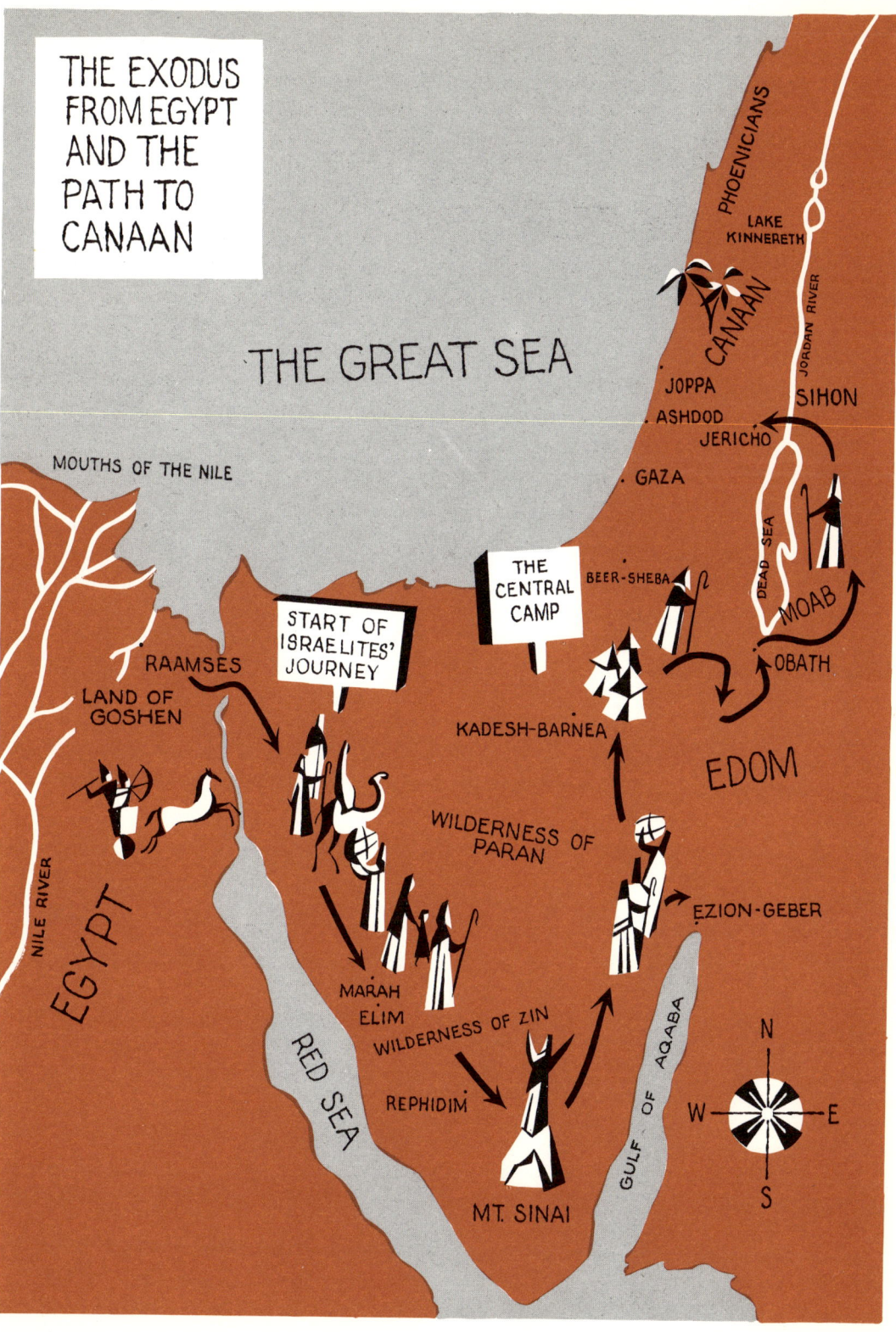

CONFIRMATION

Exercises held in some synagogues on the first day of Shavuot for young people (usually 15 or 16 years old) who have completed a course of Jewish studies, This ceremony is of recent origin.

CONSERVATIVE JUDAISM

see Judaism

COVENANT

(B'rit) the holy bond between God and man and specifically between God and Israel. The first covenant was made with Abraham. At Mount Sinai, God made the covenant with the whole people of Israel, through the Tablets of the Covenant (*Luchot HaB'rit*). Circumcision (*B'rit Milah*) is a symbol of the great Covenant.

CROWN OF THE TORAH

see Keter Torah

CUSH

Son of Ham; ancestor of the people of the land of Cush (Ethiopia).

CYRUS THE GREAT

Founder of the Persian empire, conquered Babylonia at the time of the Exile. In 538 B.C.E., he permitted and helped the Jews, led by Zerubbabel, to return to their own land and to rebuild the Temple in Jerusalem.
(Ezra, chaps. 1-3)

DAMASCUS

Ancient city and trade center in Syria; capital of a city-state whose kings often waged war against Israel. Damascus was conquered by David but was lost during the reign of Solomon.

DAN

Fifth son of Jacob; oldest son of Bilhah, ancestor of the tribe of Dan.

DANIEL

The wise man who was led into Babylonian captivity and miraculously saved from the lions' den. He interpreted the famous "writing on the wall," the Mene Tekel, at Belshazzar's feast, and predicted the end of his kingdom. Daniel's life and visions are recorded in the Book of Daniel.

DANIEL, BOOK OF

First book of historical writings in the 3rd division (*Ketubim*) of the Bible. It records the events of the life and time of Daniel and describes his visions.

DANIEL, THREE ADDITIONS TO

Books of the Apocrypha consisting of: The Prayer of Azaria and the Song of the Three Holy Children, the Story of Susanna and the Elders, and the Story of Bel and the Dragon.

DAN, TRIBE OF

One of the tribes of Israel, originally occupied a small section of central Canaan. Under Philistine pressure, the tribe moved to the most northerly part of the land. The city Dan marked the northern boundary of Israel (hence the expression, "from Dan to Beer-sheba"). Dan's banner was deep-blue; its emblem was a **serpent** and scales. The stone representing Dan in the high priest's breastplate was probably a ligure (emerald).

DARIUS I, THE GREAT

King of Persia, ruled 522-486 B.C.E. He aided and encouraged the Jews to finish the building of the Second Temple, after their return to Jerusalem from Babylonian Exile.

(Ezra, chaps. 5-6)

DATHAN

see Korah

DAVID

Son of Jesse of Bethlehem, of the tribe of Judah, descendant of Ruth, great second king of Israel who unified and strengthened the people, reigned about 1010 B.C.E. His loyal friend was Jonathan, whose father, King Saul, first cherished David and later turned against him. David conquered the Philistines and other enemies. A great warrior and religious leader, David was also a poet. He played the harp and wrote beautiful songs, recorded in the Book of Psalms and in the Books of Samuel.

DAVID, CITY OF

Another name for Jerusalem, also called Zion. David, conqueror of the Jebusite stronghold, Jerusalem, made it his capital and the religious and political center of Israel. He brought the Ark to Mount Zion. With the loyal high priest, Zadok, he instituted the first organized services and sacred music. The City of David refers specifically to the part of Jerusalem which is adjacent to Mount Zion.

DAVID, HOUSE OF

The dynasty of kings descended from David. David and Solomon ruled over all of Israel. After the division of the kingdom into Israel and Judah, the House of David ruled only over Judah, until the Babylonian Exile. Zedekiah was the last king of the House of David. The House of David ruled from about 1010-586 B.C.E.

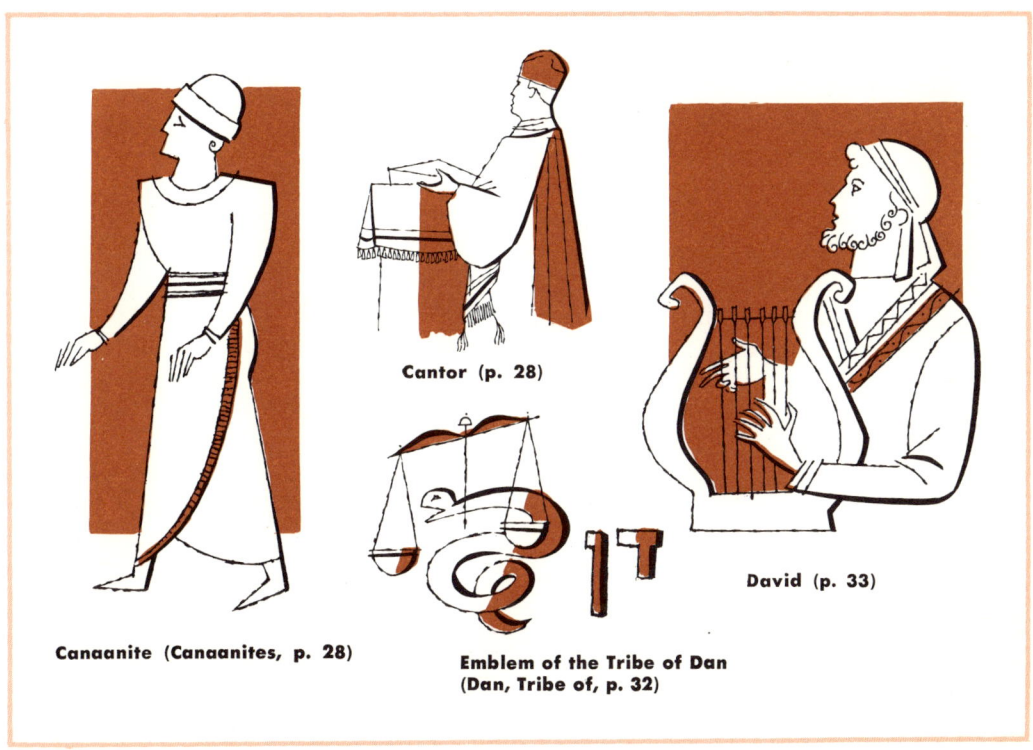

Cantor (p. 28)

Canaanite (Canaanites, p. 28)

Emblem of the Tribe of Dan
(Dan, Tribe of, p. 32)

David (p. 33)

DAYAN

A rabbi who is a judge in a rabbinical court of the Jewish community. The Dayan judges in legal and civil disputes as well as in religious and ceremonial matters.

DAY OF ATONEMENT

see Yom Kippur

DAY OF REMEMBRANCE

see Rosh Hashanah

DAYS OF AWE

(*Yamim Noraim*) refers to Rosh Hashanah and Yom Kippur.

DEAD SEA

Also called Salt Sea, or Sea of the Plain, 1,292 feet below sea level, lowest lake in the world. On its bottom lie the ruins of Sodom and Gomorrah, the evil Cities of the Plain. The important Dead Sea Scrolls, which have recently been discovered, were found near the Dead Sea.

DEBORAH

Judge and prophetess, also called Mother in Israel. She inspired Barak to conquer Sisera, the powerful leader of the Canaanites. The Song of Deborah, commemorating this victory, is one of the oldest songs in the Bible.
(Judges, chaps. 4-5)

DECALOGUE

(*Ten laws*) refers to the Ten Commandments.
see Ten Commandments

DELILAH

Samson's betrothed. She betrayed Samson to her people, the Philistines.
(Judges, chap. 16: 4-22)

DEUTERONOMY, BOOK OF

(*Devarim*) last of the Biblical Five Books of Moses (the Torah). It contains several long addresses by Moses in which he restates and explains God's commandments and laws, and in which he blesses the 12 tribes before he dies. Deuteronomy's 34 chapters are divided into 11 portions for weekly Sabbath readings. Deuteronomy is also called "Mishneh Torah" (*Repetition of the Law*).

DEVARIM

see Deuteronomy, Book of

DIASPORA

(*Dispersion*) in contrast to Galut (*exile*), refers to the more or less voluntary migration of Jews throughout the world. The term is particularly applied to the migration of Jews from the land of Israel, before the destruction of the Second Temple, to the countries of Egypt, Babylonia and Rome.

see Galut

DIETARY LAWS

The traditional laws that define which foods Jews are permitted to eat and which foods are forbidden to them, as well as the laws governing the preparation of various foods for eating. These laws can be classified into five categories:

1. Laws defining permitted (*kosher*) and forbidden (*terefah*) animals.
see Kosher

2. Laws governing ritual slaughter.
see Shehitah

3. Laws specifying portions of animals that are forbidden to eat.

4. Laws prohibiting the eating of

dairy dishes and meat dishes together.

see Milchig

see Fleishig

5. Laws governing the preparation of various foods for eating.

DINAH
Daughter of Jacob and Leah.

DREYDEL
A four-sided top used in a game played during Hanukkah. Each of the four sides of the dreydel bears one of the following Hebrew letters: Nun, Gimel, Hey, Sheen. Each person takes a turn spinning the dreydel. If it comes to Nun, the player gets nothing; Gimel, he takes all; Hey, he takes half; Sheen, he puts in. These four letters refer to the Hebrew words, Nes Gadol Hayah Sham *(a great miracle happened there)*.

see Nes Gadol Hayah Sham

ECCLESIASTES, BOOK OF
(*Kohelet*) fourth of the five Megillot of the Bible, a book of wise sayings that begins with the famous "Vanity of vanities, all is vanity . . ." This is considered to be one of three Biblical books written by King Solomon.

ECCLESIASTICUS
see Sirach

EDEN, GARDEN OF
see Garden of Eden

EDOM
see Esau

EDOMITES
Descendants of Jacob's brother Edom (Esau). Their country, Edom, was the rugged land between the Gulf of Aqaba and the Dead Sea. Edom waged many wars against Israel. Later the Greeks changed the name of Edom to Idumea. The Idumeans were defeated by Judah Maccabee, conquered and annexed to Judea by John Hyrcanus. The Herodian kings, last rulers of Judea, were Idumeans.

EGYPT
(*Mitzraim*) ancient civilization; empire on the Nile and its delta. At times of famine it was a refuge for Abraham, and later for Jacob-Israel and his sons when Joseph was second in command to Pharaoh. The tribes of Israel settled in Goshen where they eventually became slaves. Under Moses, they left Egypt and returned to the Holy Land. Powerful Egypt was the great enemy of the northern Kingdom of Israel and also of Judah, which became Egypt's vassal towards the end of its existence. Later, at the time of the destruction of the First Temple, Egypt once again became a refuge for Jews. During the Alexandrian period the city of Alexandria became a center of Jewish learning.

EHUD
Of the tribe of Benjamin; second of the Judges of Israel, a clever, left-handed hero who freed Israel from Moab's oppression.

(Judges, chap. 3: 12-30)

EIGHTEEN BENEDICTIONS
see Shemoneh Esreh

EKHAH
see Lamentations, Book of

EKRON
see Philistines

ELAH

1. The valley near Bethlehem where David slew the giant Goliath.
(Samuel I, chap. 17)
2. Fourth king of the northern Kingdom of Israel (about 890-889 B.C.E.), son of Baasa. He was assassinated by Zimri, who succeeded him for a reign of only seven days.
(Kings I, chap. 16:8-10)

ELATH

Town on the northeast corner of the Gulf of Aqaba on the Red Sea. It frequently passed back and forth between the Edomites and the Israelites. Elath and its neighboring town, ancient Ezion-Geber, were ports for Solomon's flourishing trade. Elath today is a port of the State of Israel.

ELEAZAR

1. Aaron's son and successor, second high priest of Israel.
2. Son of Mattathias, brave brother of Judah Maccabee. He died in battle, crushed by an elephant whom he had killed, thinking that he bore the tyrant, King Antiochus.

ELI

Judge and high priest in Shiloh, teacher and mentor of Samuel. Eli's sons, Hophni and Phinehas, were evil and corrupt. They died in the battle when the victorious Philistines captured the Ark. Eli died of grief. Samuel became his successor.
(Samuel I, chap. 2: 12-36; chap. 4)

ELIAKIM

see Jehoiakim

ELIEZER

Second son of Moses and Zipporah, ancestor of a group of Levites.

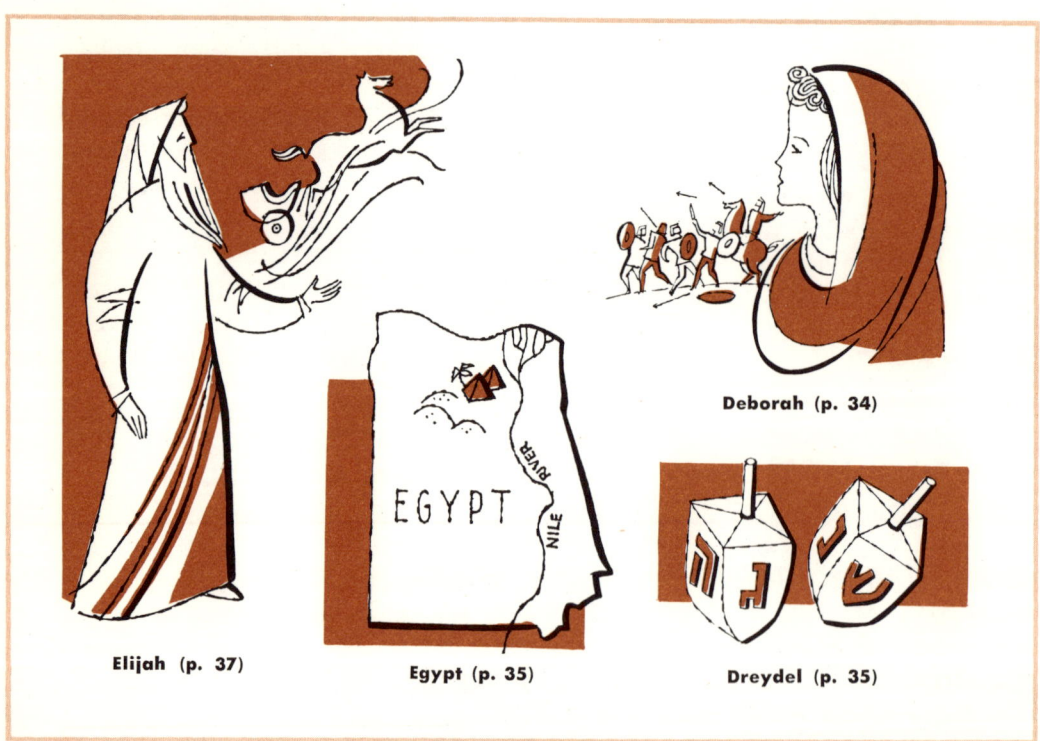

Elijah (p. 37) Egypt (p. 35) Deborah (p. 34) Dreydel (p. 35)

ELIJAH

(The Tishbite) most beloved of Israel's prophets. He courageously opposed Ahab and Jezebel and fiercely fought idol worship and the prophets of Baal. It is said that Elijah did not die an ordinary death, but, before the eyes of his faithful follower, Elisha, rose to heaven in a whirlwind. It is believed that it will be Elijah who will announce the coming of the Messiah. He is known as the helper and comforter of the poor. On Passover, during the Seder, the door is opened to the prophet Elijah and a cup is filled for him at the table. At the B'rit Milah *(circumcision)* a chair is set for Elijah.

(Kings I, chaps. 17-21; Kings II, chap. 2)

ELISHA

A prophet, successor to Elijah. An opponent of idol worship, he supported Jehu's revolt against the House of Ahab. Elisha carried on the work and preaching of Elijah. He was a healer and a performer of miracles.

(Kings I, chap. 19: 19-21; Kings II, chaps. 1-10)

ELKANAH

Husband of Hannah, father of the judge and prophet Samuel.

(Samuel I, chap. 1)

ELON

Of the tribe of Zebulun, one of the Judges of Israel. He judged for ten years.

(Judges, chap. 12: 11-12)

ELUL

Twelfth month in the Jewish calendar.

see Months, Jewish

EPHOD

Sacred garment, a short coat made of gold, blue, purple and scarlet linen worn by the high priests over their blue robes. The Ephod had two shoulder-pieces, each adorned by an onyx stone on which were engraved the names of six of Israel's twelve tribes. It was held together by an embroidered sash. The breastplate worn by the high priest was attached to the Ephod.

(Exodus, chap. 28: 1-35; chap. 39: 1-26)

EPHRAIM

Youngest son of Joseph; grandson of Jacob, ancestor of the tribe of Ephraim.

EPHRAIM, TRIBE OF

One of the tribes of Israel. It occupied the mountains of the central region of Canaan, and became the heart of the northern Kingdom of Israel, which sometimes is called, poetically, "Ephraim." Always close to its brother tribe, Manasseh, their emblems were often presented together. Ephraim's emblem was a bullock; its banner, shared with Manasseh, was jet-black. The stone representing (Manasseh and) Ephraim in the high priest's breastplate was probably an onyx.

EPHRON

The Hittite from whom Abraham bought the cave and field of Machpelah.

(Genesis, chap. 23)

EPISTLE OF JEREMIAH

see Jeremiah, Epistle of

ESAU

Also called Edom, favorite son of

Isaac, older twin of Jacob to whom he lost his birthright. Esau, who was a hunter, went to live in the region of Mount Seir, named Edom after him. His descendants were the Edomites.

(Genesis, chap. 25: 19-34; chap. 27)

ESDRAS, TWO BOOKS OF

Books of the Apocrypha, contain many excerpts from the Books of Ezra and Nehemiah. The most famous part of Esdras is the story of Darius' three young pages who, in a contest for a prize, tried to answer the question: what is the strongest thing on earth? The winning answer was: truth.

ESSENES

Jewish sect, existed in Judea from the 1st century B.C.E. through the 2nd century C.E. The Essenes were devoted to prayer and to the strict observance of Torah. They lived in monasteries — women were not allowed in their sect—sharing all possessions. Essene monasteries were concentrated in the Dead Sea region, where recently, near En Gedi, the Dead Sea Scrolls were discovered. These scrolls were probably written in an Essene community.

ESTHER

(Hadassah) cousin and ward of Mordecai, lived in Shushan, wife and queen of King Ahasuerus. Encouraged by Mordecai, she approached the mighty Ahasuerus and turned his mind against Haman's plans to kill all the Jews of Persia. These events are described in the Book of Esther and commemorated by the festival of Purim.

ESTHER, ADDITIONS TO

Book of the Apocrypha, contains additions to the Megillat Esther.

ESTHER, BOOK OF

(Megillat Esther) last of the Five Megillot of the Bible, often simply called "The Megillah." It describes how Esther saved the Jews of Persia. It is read on Purim. Many beautiful medieval Megillot, with illustrations and ornaments, mounted on hand-

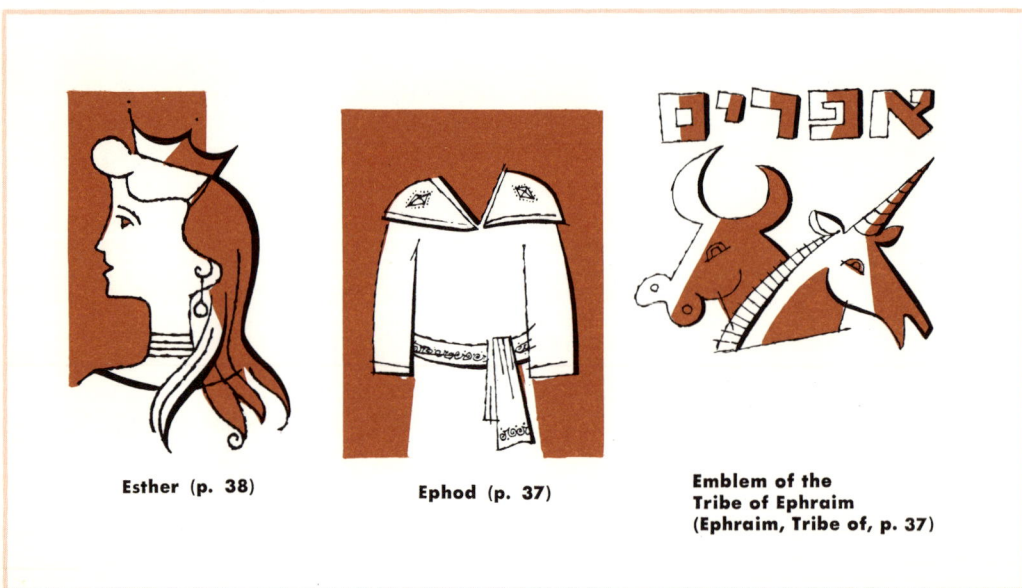

Esther (p. 38)   **Ephod (p. 37)**   **Emblem of the Tribe of Ephraim (Ephraim, Tribe of, p. 37)**

tooled or carved rollers, have been preserved.

ETERNAL LIGHT
see Ner Tamid

ETHICS OF THE FATHERS
see Pirke Avot

ETHROG
A citron or fruit resembling a lemon, one of the four plants used in the celebration of Sukkot, considered one of the most beautiful fruits of ancient Israel.

(Lev., chap. 23:40)

see Sukkot, Four Plants of

ETZ HAYIM
Symbolic name of the Torah and specifically the name of the wooden rollers to which the ends of the Torah scrolls are attached. The term means "tree of life" and is derived from the saying, "It (the Torah) is a tree of life to those who uphold it."

EVE
First woman, wife of Adam, mother of Cain, Abel and Seth.

see Adam and Eve

(Genesis, chaps. 2-3)

EVENING SERVICE
see Maariv

EXILARCH
(Leader of the Exile) the worldly leader of the Babylonian Jews, a hereditary office from about the 2nd century to about the 13th century C.E. Exilarchs held court, appointed officials and collected taxes. It was said that the Exilarchs were descendants of the royal House of David.

EXILE, BABYLONIAN
The forced stay of the Jews in Babylonia (about 586-538 B.C.E.) away from their homeland. It occurred after Nebuchadnezzar's victory over Judah and the destruction of the First Temple. Captives from Judah were deported to cultivate agricultural regions of the Babylonian provinces and some were sent to the city of Babylon itself.

EXODUS
(Yetziat Mitzraim) the going out from Egypt of the Israelites, under Moses' guidance, to the Promised Land.

EXODUS, BOOK OF
(Shemot) second of the Biblical Five Books of Moses (the Torah). It relates the experiences of the Israelites in Egypt, the birth of Moses, his mission and the Exodus from Egypt. It includes chapters on the giving of the Ten Commandments at Mount Sinai and the building of the Tabernacle and the Ark. Exodus' 40 chapters are divided into 11 portions for weekly Sabbath readings.

EZEKIEL
Third of the Major Prophets, lived in the 6th century B.C.E., at the time of the Babylonian Exile. His words are recorded in the Biblical Book of Ezekiel. Ezekiel explained the meaning of the Exile. He gave the people faith, comfort and hope, and prophesied the rebuilding of Jerusalem and the Temple.

EZEKIEL, BOOK OF
Third of the Books of the three Major Prophets of the Bible. It contains the words of the prophet Ezekiel.

EZION-GEBER

Important port at the time of Solomon. Solomon's famous copper mines were excavated near this site.
see Elath

EZRA

Priest, scribe and teacher who returned to Jerusalem from Babylon, and, with the aid of Nehemiah, helped restore the strength of the Jewish community of Judea. Ezra is regarded as the first of the Soferim (scribes) and the founder of the rabbinic tradition. His life and works are recorded in the Books of Ezra and Nehemiah.

EZRA, BOOK OF

With the Book of Nehemiah, the second book of historical writings of the 3rd division *(Ketubim)* of the Bible. The book records the major events in the life of Ezra and his teachings.

FALASHAS

Dark-skinned Jews of northwestern Abyssinia, claim to be descendants of Israelites who returned with the Queen of Sheba from Solomon's court. Falashas observe variations of ancient Jewish rituals. There are Falasha synagogues in the United States.

FAST DAYS

Jews fast to express repentance or as a sign of mourning. But the main purpose of fasting is to enable man to commune better with God. In addition to the fast day of Yom Kippur, there are also commemorative fast days, of which the four best known are: Tisha B'Av, Taanit Esther, Tzom Gedaliah and Asarah Betevet.

FAST OF ESTHER

see Taanit Esther

FAST OF GEDALIAH

see Tzom Gedaliah

FAST OF (THE 17th DAY OF) TAMMUZ

see Shivah Asar Betammuz

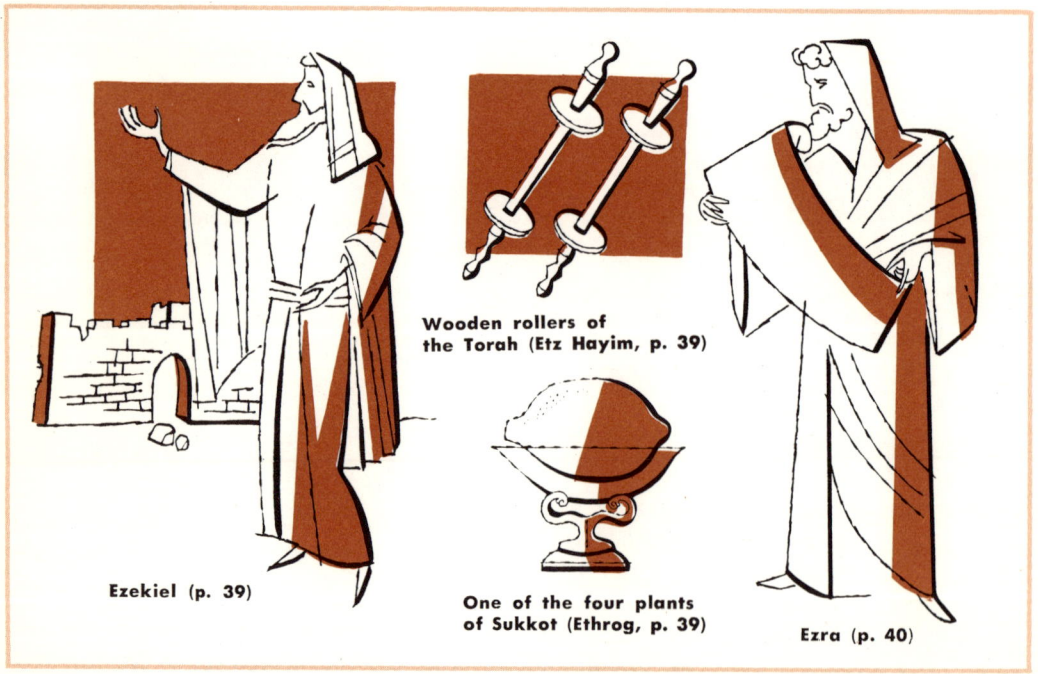

Ezekiel (p. 39)

Wooden rollers of the Torah (Etz Hayim, p. 39)

One of the four plants of Sukkot (Ethrog, p. 39)

Ezra (p. 40)

FAST OF THE FIRST-BORN
see Taanit Behorim

FAST OF THE TENTH OF TEVET
see Asarah Betevet

FAST OF THE NINTH OF AV
see Tisha B'Av

FEAST OF FREEDOM
see Passover

FEAST OF LIGHTS
see Hanukkah

FEAST OF LOTS
see Purim

FEAST OF TABERNACLES
see Sukkot

FEAST OF WEEKS
see Shavuot

FERTILE CRESCENT
Modern term for the crescent formed by the fertile lands along the fringe of the Arabian desert, starting in the northeast at the Persian Gulf and including the lands watered by the great rivers: the Tigris and Euphrates (Babylonia, Assyria, Persia), the Jordan (Syria, Phoenicia, Israel), and the Nile (Egypt). Through the Fertile Crescent, Abraham, the Patriarch, and all the great peoples of antiquity have traveled.

FIRST BORN, REDEMPTION OF
see Pidyon Haben

FIVE BOOKS OF MOSES
see Humash

FIVE MEGILLOT
see Megillot, Five

FLEISHIG
Food derived from the meat of mammals and poultry. The Jewish dietary laws prohibit the eating of meat and milk products together and require separate cooking and table utensils for the preparation and eating of each of the two kinds of food.
see Milchig

FOUR MOTHERS
Also called Matriarchs, the wives of Israel's Patriarchs: Sarah, Rebekah, Leah and Rachel.

FOUR QUESTIONS
see Mah Nishtanah

FRINGES
The custom of wearing fringes on the garments of Jewish men dates back to very ancient times. They are worn in fulfillment of the Biblical commandment to wear them as a reminder of God's commandments. Fringes are worn on the Tallit and the Arba Kanfot.
(Numbers, chap. 15:37-41)

FRONTLETS
see Tefillin

GABIROL, SOLOMON IBN
see Ibn Gabirol, Solomon

GABRIEL
Angel and messenger of God. He and Michael are considered the protectors of Israel.

GAD
Seventh son of Jacob; oldest son of Zilpah, ancestor of the tribe of Gad.

GAD, TRIBE OF

One of the tribes of Israel. Its territory was the mountainous terrain east of the Jordan. The emblem of Gad was an encampment of tents; its banner was grey. The stone representing Gad in the high priest's breastplate was probably an agate.

GALUT

(*Exile*) refers to the compulsory exile of Jews from the land of Israel after the destruction of the Second Temple.

see Diaspora.

GAMALIEL I

Grandson or son of Hillel; Nasi and last head of the Sanhedrin before the destruction of the Second Temple. Gamaliel was the first to be called "Rabban" (*our teacher*). He was a man of great wisdom and piety. His judgments were lenient and always for the common good. He was beloved by the community of Judea.

GAMALIEL II

Rabban Gamaliel of Javneh; grandson of Gamaliel I; Nasi, head of the academy and Sanhedrin at Javneh, leader of the people after the destruction of the Temple (80-110 C.E.). His sternness was often criticized, but he was selflessly devoted to the unity of the Jewish community.

GAN EDEN

see Garden of Eden

GA'ON

(*Eminence, Excellency*) the title of the presidents of the Babylonian academies, Sura and Pumpadita, after the close of the Talmudic period. The Ga'onim (plural) were recognized as the spiritual heads of Judaism. The time of the Ga'onim is called the Ga'onic period (late 6th to 11th centuries C.E.).

GARDEN OF EDEN

(*Gan Eden*) the Biblical name for the peaceful, idyllic, original home of Adam and Eve. The Garden of Eden is also called Paradise.

(Genesis, chap. 2: 8-18)

GATH

see Philistines

GAZA

Ancient city, port of the Philistines. David, fleeing from Saul, found refuge in Gaza.

see Philistines

GEDALIAH

Son of Ahikam; friend and protector of Jeremiah, installed by Nebuchadnezzar as governor of Judea after the destruction of the First Temple. Gedaliah tried to reunite the scattered people of Judah. He was assassinated by Ishmael, prince of the House of David. Gedaliah's death hastened the Babylonian Exile. His death is commemorated by the Fast of Gedaliah (*Tzom Gedaliah*), on the 3rd of Tishri.

(Kings II, chap. 25: 22-26; Jeremiah, chaps. 40-41)

GELILAH

The "rolling up" of the Torah scroll after it has been read. The person who receives the honor to perform the Gelilah is called the Golel (*he who rolls up*).

GEMARA

(*Study, learning*) second part of the

Talmud, consists of discussions and commentaries on its first and basic part, the Mishnah. The Gemara, compiled (third to sixth centuries, C.E.), after the completion of the Mishnah, consists of the teachings of the Amoraim. Two distinct versions are in existence, the Palestinian and the Babylonian Gemara.

GENESIS, BOOK OF

(*Bereshit*) first of the Biblical Five Books of Moses (the Torah). Genesis relates the origins of Israel, from the Creation to the death of Joseph. Its 50 chapters are divided into 12 portions for weekly Sabbath readings. The Hebrew name for Genesis (*Bereshit*) is the first word in the book and means "in the beginning."

GENIZAH

(*Hiding place*) a storeroom, usually in a synagogue, for Torah scrolls and other sacred writings that become unfit for use. Recent discoveries of ancient storerooms have provided scholars with invaluable historical information.

GENTILES

Persons who are not Jewish by birth and religion. The word does not refer to a person's race or nationality but to his religious belief.

GERIZIM, MOUNT

The mountain, designated by Moses as a place of assembly and blessing, where Joshua and other leaders of Israel blessed the people. At its foot was the ancient city of Shechem (now Nablus). On Mount Gerizim stood the Temple of the Samaritans, built in the 4th century B.C.E., and destroyed by John Hyrcanus (about 128 B.C.E.). Today the Samaritans still celebrate Passover on Mount Gerizim.

(Deut., chap. 11:29; Joshua, chap. 8:30-35)

GERSHOM

Oldest son of Moses and Zipporah.

GET

(*Bill of divorcement*) a religious divorce. In traditional Jewish life a civil divorce must be followed by the granting of a religious document of divorce.

GHETTO

The section of a city in which Jews were compelled to live by law. The compulsory ghetto for Jews existed in many parts of Europe during the 13th to 18th centuries. The ghetto was revived in recent times by the Nazis.

GIBEAH

Home and capital of King Saul, in the territory of Benjamin, near Jerusalem. Parts of Gibeah, including Saul's dwelling, have been excavated by modern archeologists.

GIDEON

Also called Jerubbaal, of the tribe of Manasseh, one of the most important Judges who ruled in Israel (12th century B.C.E.). He zealously fought idol worship in Israel and battled the hostile neighboring tribes. With 300 men he defeated the powerful Midianites in a surprise attack. He helped unite the tribes of Israel and strengthened them in their belief in One God.

(Judges, chaps. 6-8)

GILBOA, MOUNT

Mountain in Galilee, southeast of the

Emek Jezreel, where Saul and Jonathan died in the great battle they lost to the Philistines.

(Samuel I, chap. 31)

GILEAD

The beautiful and fertile land of the Jabbok River, east of the Jordan and south of the Yarmuk, where the tribes of Gad and Reuben (and for a period Manasseh) settled; home of Jephthah and Elijah. Since the time of the Patriarchs, many Biblical events took place in Gilead.

GILGAL

A town between Jericho and Jerusalem. The Israelites, under Joshua, set up their first camp site in Gilgal after they had crossed the Jordan.

(Joshua, chap. 4: 19-24)

GOLAN

City of Refuge, in the territory of Manasseh.

see Cities of Refuge

GOLEL

see Gelilah

GOLIATH

A giant soldier in the Philistine army defeated by the young David. David killed the heavily armed Goliath with only a slingshot and so won a great victory for Israel.

(Samuel I, chap. 17)

Emblem of the Tribe of Gad
(Gad, Tribe of, p. 42)

The wearing of Fringes
(Fringes, p. 41)

David and Goliath
(Goliath, p. 44)

Gate of a medieval European ghetto
(Ghetto, p. 43)

GOLUS
Ashkenazic pronunciation of Galut.
see Galut

GOMORRAH
One of the five Cities of the Plain. It was destroyed because of the wickedness of its people.
see Sodom

GOSHEN
Grazing ground in the land of Egypt, near the Sinai Peninsula, that Pharaoh gave to Jacob and his family. At that time, Jacob's son, Joseph, was second in command to Pharaoh in Egypt. The Exodus of the Israelites from Egypt started from Goshen.
(Genesis, chap. 47: 1-6)

GRACE AFTER MEALS
(*Birkat Hamazon*) a prayer of ancient origin recited by many Jews after meals.

GRACE BEFORE MEALS
see Hamotzi

GREAT SANHEDRIN
see Sanhedrin, the Great

GREGGER
A noisemaker used in the celebration of Purim.

GUT SHABBOS
Greeting meaning "a good and happy Sabbath."

GUT YOM TOV
Greeting meaning "a good and happy holiday."

HABAKKUK
Eighth of the Books of Twelve (Minor) Prophets of the Bible. Little is known about the prophet himself. In addition to recording his prophecies, he explored the problem of why a wicked man may succeed and a righteous man may suffer. He concluded that man must be just and have faith in God, for He will make the final judgment.

HADAS
(*Myrtle*) one of the four plants used in the celebration of Sukkot.
(Lev., chap. 23: 40)
see Sukkot, Four Plants of

HADASSAH
Hebrew name for Esther.
see Esther

HAD GADYAH
(*One Kid*) the title of a ballad sung at the conclusion of the Seder celebration.

HAFTARAH
(*Conclusion*) passages from the Prophetic books read in the synagogue after the reading from the Torah. The Haftarah is read on Sabbath, special days and holidays. The Bar or Bat Mitzvah is often honored by being called to read from the Haftarah.

HAGAR
Maid of Sarah; mother of Ishmael. She and her son were cast out of Abraham's household and sent into the wilderness of Beer-sheba.
(Genesis, chap. 16; chap. 21: 9-21)

HAGBAAH
"The Lifting Up" of the Torah to the congregation by a worshipper who is

thus honored, usually at the conclusion of the reading.

HAGGADAH
see Aggadah

HAGGADAH, PASSOVER
The text of the home service read during the Seder ceremony. It contains stories *(Haggadah)*, and prayers and songs praising God for his deliverance of the Jews from Egyptian slavery. Many editions are beautifully printed and illustrated.

HAGGAI
Tenth of the Books of Twelve (Minor) Prophets. The prophet Haggai, after returning to Jerusalem from Babylonian Exile, inspired Zerubbabel and the high priest Joshua to build the Second Temple.

HAGIOGRAPHA
The Greek name for Ketubim, the third division of the Bible.

see Ketubim

HAG SAMEAH
Greeting used on holidays, meaning "a happy holiday."

HAKAFOT
(Rounds) processions with the Torah around the Bimah and the synagogue on Simhat Torah. All the Torah scrolls are taken from the Ark and the men of the congregation take

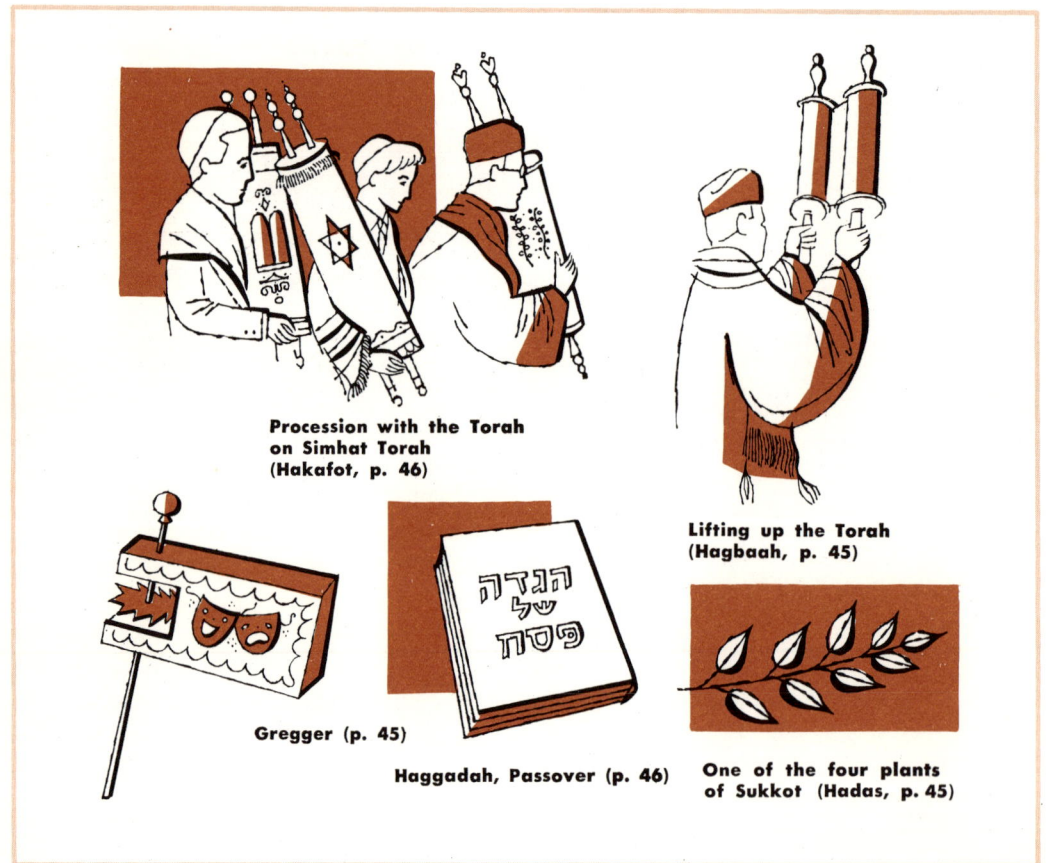

Procession with the Torah on Simhat Torah (Hakafot, p. 46)

Lifting up the Torah (Hagbaah, p. 45)

Gregger (p. 45)

Haggadah, Passover (p. 46)

One of the four plants of Sukkot (Hadas, p. 45)

turns carrying them, singing psalms and prayers. Children, waving flags, join the joyous processions.

HALACHAH

(*The proper way*) the discussions, commentaries and decisions on Jewish civil and religious law that form a basic part of the Talmud. Halachah, in contrast to Aggadah, is the legal part of the Talmud.

see Aggadah

HALEVI, JUDAH

see Judah Halevi

HALLAH

A white bread generally baked in a braided shape. It is usually served at all Sabbath and holiday meals to make these occasions more festive.

HALLEL

Psalms of praise and prayer, recited between Shemoneh Esreh and the reading of the Torah on the Three Festivals, Rosh Hodesh and Hanukkah.

HAM

One of the three sons of Noah. According to Biblical tradition he is the ancestor of the African peoples.

HAMAN

Prime minister and favorite of King Ahasuerus, plotted to destroy the Jews of Persia. Queen Esther went to the mighty Ahasuerus and exposed Haman's plans. Haman was hanged and the Jews of Persia were saved. The holiday of Purim celebrates this event.

HAMANTASHEN

Three-cornered pastries filled with poppy seeds or prunes, traditionally served on Purim. Hamantashen is a Yiddish word meaning "Haman's pockets."

HAMETZ

(*Leavened bread*) during Passover all leavened food is removed from the home. Traditionally, Jews do not eat leavened food during Passover or use dishes and utensils employed during the rest of the year.

HAMISHAH ASAR BISHVAT

(*The Fifteenth Day of the Month of Shevat*), also called Tu Bishvat, a holiday also known as Jewish Arbor Day. In Israel, this holiday signifies the beginning of spring. It is customary for this day to be observed by tree-planting ceremonies.

HAMOTZI

The words of the blessing over the bread which mean "Who brings forth." As bread is the most basic food, the Hamotzi grace is the customary one recited before meals.

HANASI, JUDAH

see Judah Hanasi

HANNAH

1. Wife of Elkanah. Her prayers for a son, at the sanctuary of Shiloh, were fulfilled. She became the mother of the great judge and prophet Samuel.
(**Samuel I, chaps. 1-2**)
2. Martyr who lived under the reign of Antiochus IV of Syria, at the time preceding the Maccabean revolt. Hannah's seven sons bravely gave their lives rather than forsake their Jewish heritage.

HANUKKAH

A holiday lasting eight days. It commemorates the rededication of the ancient Temple in Jerusalem by Judah Maccabee and his followers who defeated Antiochus. The lighting of candles on Hanukkah is a reminder of the miracle of the tiny jug of oil that burned for eight days and eight nights. Hannukah means "dedication." Hanukkah is also called "Feast of Lights."

HARAN

1. Brother of Abraham; son of Terah, father of Lot.

2. Ancient city in Paddan-Aram (Mesopotamia) where Abraham left his kin to go to the Promised Land. Haran was the home of Rebekah, Rachel and Leah.

HAROSET

A mixture of apples, nuts, cinnamon and wine. It is eaten at the Passover Seder as a reminder of the mortar with which the Jews were forced to make bricks when they were slaves in Egypt.

HASID

Deeply religious and compassionate person.

HASIDEANS

(*Hasidim*) Jewish party (sect) at the time of the Maccabees. The Hasideans upheld the Jewish tradition and way of life against the influence of Greek ideas.

Hamantashen (p. 47)

Hamishah Asar Bishvat (page 47)

Hanukkah (p. 48)

Hallah (p. 47)

Haman (p. 47)

HASIDISM

Religious movement founded in the Ukraine in the 18th century by Israel Ben Eliezer, called the Baal Shem Tov. It spread quickly over Eastern Europe. Today its followers live all over the world. Hasidism, founded on the mystical ideas of the Cabala, believes that to serve God is a great joy. All men and all things, Hasidim believe, are inhabited by the Shekhinah, a part of God; it is for man to uncover it. Hasidism has a rich tradition of songs, legends and writings.

HASKALAH

(*Enlightenment*) Jewish movement that brought the culture and ideas of the 19th century non-Jewish world into the ghettos of Germany and Austria, and later of Poland, Russia and other Eastern European countries. The Haskalah contributed to the breakdown of the ghettos and to the establishment of rights heretofore denied to the Jews. It also inspired a flowering of modern Hebrew and Yiddish culture.

HASMONEAN DYNASTY

The reign of priests and kings (141-37 B.C.E.) established by the high priest, Simon, and by his son, John Hyrcanus I. The first Hasmonean to assume the title of king was Aristobulus I and the last was Antigonus (Mattathiah), who was executed by the Romans and succeeded by Herod.

see chart, p. 50

HASMONEANS

Also called Maccabees, descendants of Hashmon, great-grandfather of Mattathias who with his five sons, the Maccabees, led the revolt against Antiochus. Judah was the leader of the Maccabees. After Judah's death, his brother, Simon, became the head of Judea and high priest.

HATAN

see Hatunah

HATAN BERESHIT

(*Bridegroom of Bereshit*) the person honored by being called to the reading of the first portion (Bereshit) of the Torah on Simhat Torah, when the reading of the Torah begins anew.

HATAN TORAH

(*Bridegroom of the Torah*) the person honored by being called on Simhat Torah to the reading of the concluding portion of the Torah.

HATIKVAH

Anthem of the Zionists and the State of Israel, based on a poem by Naphtali Hertz Imber. Hatikvah means "The Hope."

HATUNAH

Ceremony and celebration of a wedding. The groom is called Hatan; the bride is called Kallah.

HAVDALAH

(*Separation*) a ceremony that observes the end of the Sabbath or a festival. Wine, a spice box (Besamim box), and a braided candle are used in the ceremony that marks the separation of the sacredness of the Sabbath or festival from the ordinary workday.

HAZAN

see Cantor

HEBREW

(*Ivrit*) the language of the Bible and of ancient Israel, part of the Semitic language group, related to Aramaic and Arabic, also called Leshon Hakodesh (*holy language*). Hebrew, like all Semitic languages, is written from right to left and consisted originally, in writing, only of consonants. Modern Hebrew, language of the State of Israel, uses the Sephardic pronunciation. The Ashkenazic pronunciation of Hebrew, however, is still used in many synagogues and schools.

HEBREWS

A name occasionally applied to Israelites by people of other nations. Today "Hebrews" is sometimes used as a term to designate the Israelites from the time of Jacob's death to the Exodus from Egypt. The Hebrews were later called Israelites and eventually Jews.

HEBREW SCHOOL

Usually refers to afternoon religious schools which meet after the public school session. These schools are usually conducted under the auspices of the synagogue.

HEBRON

One of the most ancient towns of Palestine, home of the Patriarchs, Abra-

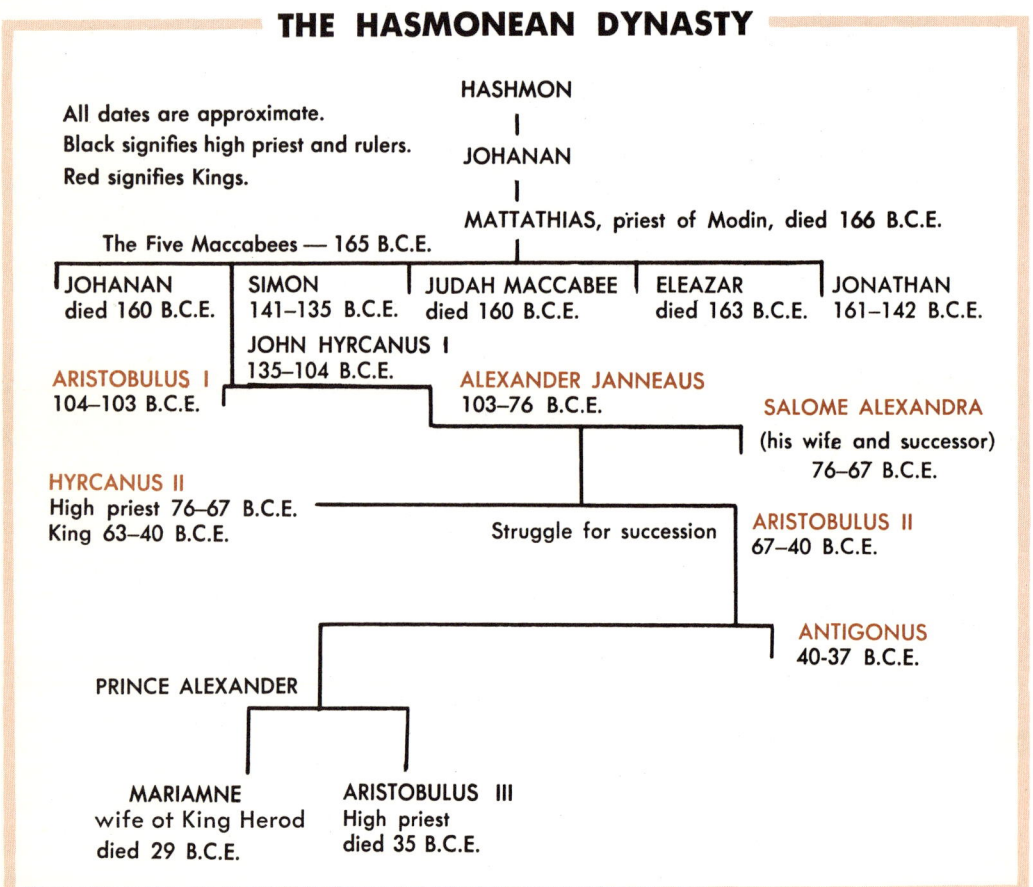

ham, Isaac and Jacob. The town is either identical with or very near ancient Mamre. Near Hebron is the Cave of Machpelah, where the Patriarchs were buried. Hebron, in the territory of Judah, was one of the Cities of Refuge. It was David's capital, until his conquest of Jerusalem. Hebron is now in Arab territory.

HEDER

Usually a one-room school, privately owned, often in the home of a teacher, where children receive an elementary Jewish religious education. This form of religious instruction has declined in the United States.

HELLENISM

The ideas, religion and way of life of the ancient Greeks, carried and propagated throughout the ancient world by Alexander the Great.

HEROD

Idumean king of Judea, installed by the Romans. He destroyed and supplanted the Hasmonean dynasty, executing his own wife, the beautiful Hasmonean princess Mariamne. This tyrannical king, despite his cruelty, is said to have been a cultured man. He built many magnificient structures in Jerusalem, and is especially remembered for beautifying and enlarging the Second Temple. Herod ruled from 37 to 4 B.C.E.

HERODIAN DYNASTY

The royal House of Herod (of Idumean origin), last kings of Judea before its destruction by the Romans. The Herodians were: Herod, son of Antipater; Herod's sons, Archelaus and Antipas (also called Herod Antipas); Herod's grandson, Agrippa I and his great-grandson, Agrippa II. The Herodians ruled from about 37 B.C.E.-70 C.E.

HESHVAN

Second month in the Jewish calendar, also called Mar-Heshvan.

see Months, Jewish

HEZEKIAH

Thirteenth king of Judah; son of Ahaz, reigned about 720-692 B.C.E. After Assyria destroyed Israel, he supplied Jerusalem with an adequate water system and strengthened its fortifications just before the long Assyrian siege of the city. Hezekiah prayed for delivery while the prophet Isaiah inspired the besieged people to hold out. The Assyrians, beset by plague and other difficulties, withdrew from Jerusalem.

(Kings II, chaps. 18-20; Isaiah, chaps. 36-39)

HIGH HOLY DAYS

see Rosh Hashanah

see Yom Kippur

HIGH PRIEST

The highest office in the priestly class (*Cohanim*), a hereditary office. The high priest lived by the Priestly Code, performing the most sacred tasks in the Temple. He alone was allowed to enter the Holy of Holies once a year, on Yom Kippur, to pray for all the people of Israel. Aaron was the first high priest.

HILKIAH

High priest in the time of King Josiah. He helped the king restore the religious faith of the people.

(Kings II, chaps. 22-23)

HILLEL

Great scholar and teacher of the 1st century B.C.E., one of the founders of Oral Torah, colleague and opponent of Shammai. Hillel, who was born in Babylonia, studied in Jerusalem, where he lived in poverty. He won many disciples. He rose to Nasi, the head of the Sanhedrin, a position and title inherited by his family. Discussions between Hillel and Shammai (his Av Bet Din), and their schools are recorded in the Mishnah. Hillel, unlike the quick-tempered Shammai, was lenient and gentle. His golden rule, which he believed to be the foundation of Judaism, was to love one's neighbor as one self.

see Zugot

HILLEL II

Nasi, formulated the Jewish calendar which, until his time, the 4th century C.E., had been secretly calculated each year and was proclaimed by messengers to the Jews of the various lands. The present Jewish calendar is based on the formulation of Hillel II.

HIRAM

Phoenician king of Tyre, friend and ally of King Solomon.

(Kings I, chap. 5: 1-12)

HITTITES

Powerful, warlike people of ancient Canaan. They had a highly developed civilization and had ruled over

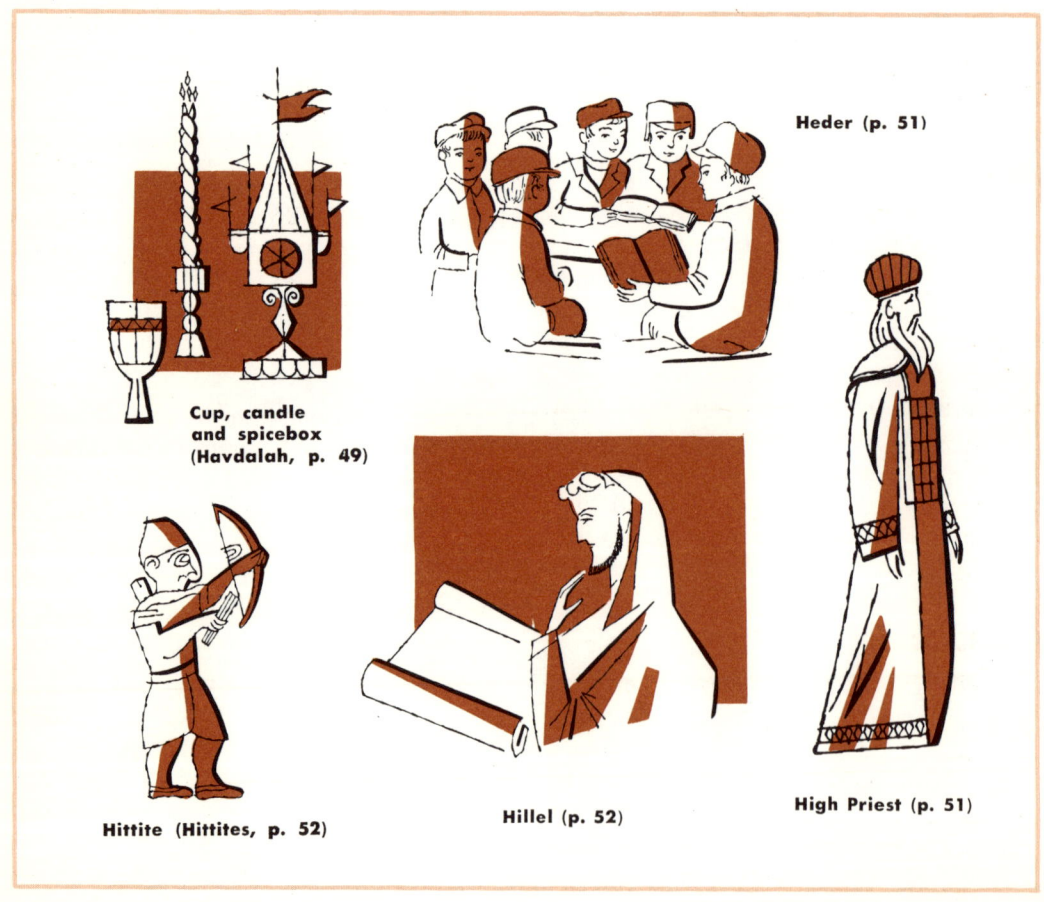

Cup, candle and spicebox (Havdalah, p. 49)

Heder (p. 51)

Hittite (Hittites, p. 52)

Hillel (p. 52)

High Priest (p. 51)

a great empire (about 2000 B.C.E.). They were eventually conquered by the Assyrians.

HODESH
see Month

HOL HAMOED
Weekday of the holiday. It refers to the days between the first and last days of both the holidays of Passover and Sukkot. These days are half-holidays; services are held but the everyday work-tasks can be performed.

HOLY LAND
Israel, the Promised Land, the land promised to Abraham, Isaac, Jacob-Israel and to their descendants, the people of Israel.

see Canaan

see Israel

HOLY OF HOLIES
(*Kodesh Hakodashim*) the most holy place in the Tabernacle, and later in the Temple, where the Ark of the Covenant was kept. The Holy of Holies was entered only by the high priest, once a year, on the holy day of Yom Kippur.

HOPHNI
One of the sons of the Judge and high priest Eli, regarded unworthy to succeed his father. Hophni and his brother Phinehas fell in the battle against the Philistines, when the Ark was captured.

(Samuel I, chap. 2: 12-35; chap. 4: 11-22)

HOR, MOUNT
A mountain near the coast of Edom and Kadesh-barnea where the Israelites' camp site stood. Aaron died at Mount Hor.

(Numbers, chap. 20: 22-29)

HOREB, MOUNT
Biblical name of Mount Sinai, in Deuteronomy.

see Sinai, Mount

HOSEA
First of the Books of Twelve (Minor) Prophets of the Bible. The prophet Hosea wrote and preached in the 8th century B.C.E. in Israel, at the time of Jeroboam II and the disorder that followed the king's death. He preached against the immorality of his day, reminding the people that God wants men to be just and compassionate.

HOSHANAH RABBAH
The seventh day of the Sukkot holiday. It is observed in the synagogue by seven processions around the pulpit, accompanied by chanting Hoshanah (a prayer for God's help and salvation), and the waving of palm branches. The concluding prayers (Hoshanot) are traditionally accompanied by the beating of Hoshanot (willow-branches) against the ground and benches.

HOSHANOT
1. The Hoshanah prayers of Hoshanah Rabbah.

2. The willow-branches used on Hoshanah Rabbah during the prayer for rain and salvation. In ancient Israel, the willow was a symbol for the fruitfulness of rain.

see Aravah

HOSHEA
Last king of the northern Kingdom of Israel (about 734-722 B.C.E.). He allied Israel with Egypt, ignoring earlier treaties with powerful Assyria.

Shalmaneser, the Assyrian king, and Sargon II, his successor, overran Israel. Samaria, the capital, held out against a siege that lasted three years. After its fall, Hoshea was taken prisoner and the ten tribes of the Kingdom of Israel were led into captivity and scattered over the lands.

(Kings II, chap. 17: 1-23)

HULDAH

Prophetess, advisor to King Josiah. She was consulted to interpret the meanings of the lost book of the Torah that was found in the Temple during Josiah's reign. Huldah helped Josiah rekindle the people's religious faith.

(Kings II, chap. 22: 14-20)

HUMASH

Short form of Hamisha Humshe Torah (the five-fifths of the Torah). The Humash is the book containing the Five Books of Moses and the Prophetic passages read each week in the synagogue. The Five Books of Moses are: Genesis *(Bereshit)*, Exodus *(Shemot)*, Leviticus *(Vayikra)*, Numbers *(Bamidbar)* and Deuteronomy *(Devarim)*.

HUPPAH

Wedding-canopy, consisting of a square top cover, often made of silk or satin, supported by four poles which either stand on the ground or are held during the ceremony by four young men. The bride and the bridegroom are wed under the Huppah.

see Hatunah

HUR

Assistant to Moses, who, with Aaron, supported Moses' uplifted hands while he prayed for victory during the battle against the Amalekites. Some say he was the husband of Miriam.

(Exodus, chap. 17: 8-16)

HYRCANUS I, JOHN

(Johanan) Hasmonean high priest and ruler of Judea (about 135-104 B.C.E.), son of the high priest Simon. After a long struggle he achieved Judean independence from Syria. He extended and fortified the borders of Judea. Intolerant of other religions, he destroyed the Temple of the Samaritans on Mount Gerizim, and he forcibly converted the Idumeans to Judaism.

HYRCANUS II

Hasmonean high priest (about 76-67 B.C.E.), son of Alexander Janneaus and Salome Alexandra, became king of Judea (67), but was dethroned by his brother Aristobulus II. The two brothers' bitter fight for the succession brought about the fall of the Hasmonean house and the end of Judea's independence.

IBN EZRA

1. (Abraham) writer of famous Bible commentaries, grammarian, philosopher, astrologer and poet. He lived in Spain and Italy (about 1092-1167 C.E.).

2. (Moses) probably brother of Abraham, great poet, lived in Granada, Spain (died about 1139). He wrote in both Hebrew and Arabic.

IBN GABIROL, SOLOMON

Great philosopher and poet, lived in Spain, about 1021-1058 C.E. He wrote many great works, in both Hebrew and Arabic.

IBZAN

Of Bethlehem, one of the Judges of Israel. He judged for seven years.
(Judges, chap. 12: 8-10)

IDUMEA

see Edomites

IRAN

see Persia

IRAQ

see Mesopotamia

ISAAC

Second of the Patriarchs, son of Abraham, husband of Rebekah, father of Jacob and Esau. The most famous incident in Isaac's life is the Akedah (*binding*), when Isaac was bound on the altar by Abraham. God tested Abraham by asking him to sacrifice his son and only heir. Abraham and Isaac were willing to obey God's command, but God intended only a test of Abraham's faith and sent an angel to intervene. A ram was sacrificed instead of Isaac and God renewed His covenant with Abraham (and his descendants). Isaac, a successful farmer and cattle-breeder, was a pious man. He lived in Mamre (Hebron) and was buried in the Cave of Machpelah.
(Genesis, chap. 22)

ISAIAH

First of the Major Prophets. His words are recorded in the Book of Isaiah of the Bible. He lived during the reigns of Uzziah, Jotham, Ahaz and Hezekiah. Isaiah, son of Amoz, prophesied the destruction of Judah, but also foresaw Israel's reconstruction and a future time of peace and brotherhood throughout the world, when "Men shall beat their swords into plowshares . . . neither shall they learn war anymore . . ."
(Isaiah, chap. 2: 4)

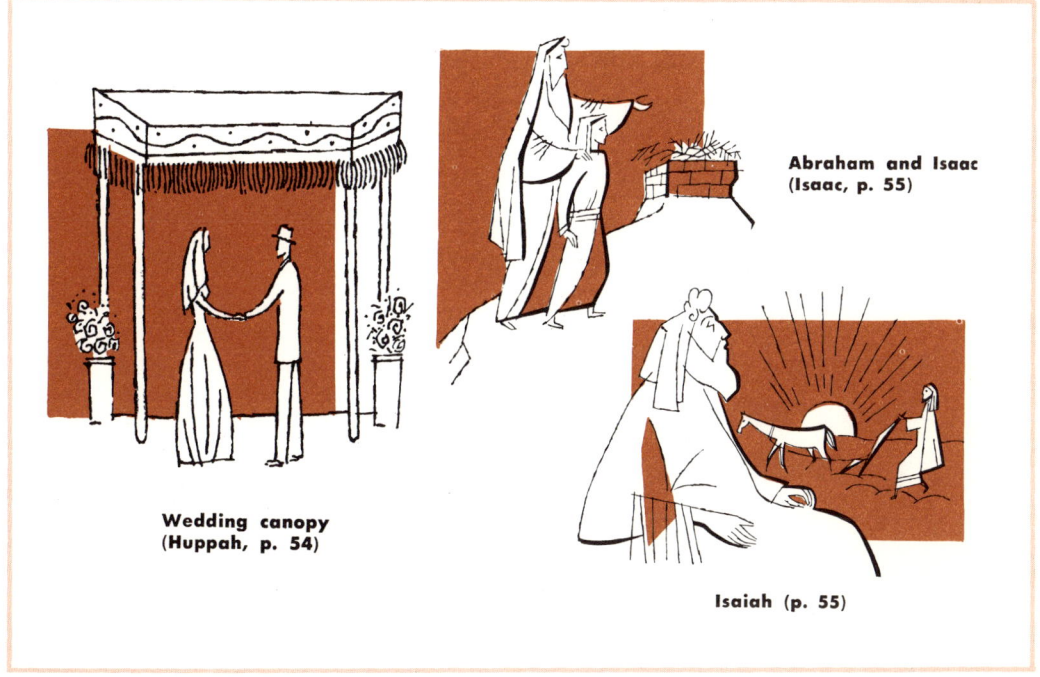

Wedding canopy (Huppah, p. 54)

Abraham and Isaac (Isaac, p. 55)

Isaiah (p. 55)

ISAIAH, BOOK OF
First of the Books of the three Major Prophets of the Bible. It contains the words of the prophet Isaiah.

ISHBAAL
see Ish-bosheth

ISH-BOSHETH
Also called Ishbaal, fourth son of King Saul. After Saul's death he ruled over part of Israel, while David ruled over the tribe of Judah. Ish-bosheth reigned for about two years.
(Samuel II, chap. 4)

ISHMAEL
Son of Abraham and Hagar. He was cast out of Abraham's household with his mother and sent into the wilderness of Beer-sheba. He is the ancestor of the Arabs and an important figure in Islamic writings.
(Genesis, chap. 16; chap. 21: 9-21)

ISRAEL
The name given to Jacob—"he who strove with God"—eventually became the name for the people of Israel as a whole. Israel became the name for the northern Kingdom in particular, but it continued to be the national and religious name for the entire Jewish people.
(Genesis, chap. 32: 23-30)

ISRAEL BEN ELIEZER
Founder of Hasidism
see Baal Shem Tov

ISRAEL, KINGDOM OF
Founded by Saul about 1040 B.C.E., succeeding kings were David and Solomon. The Kingdom was divided (about 937 B.C.E.) at the time of Rehoboam, Solomon's son, into the northern Kingdom of Israel and the southern Kingdom of Judah. The northern Kingdom, founded by King Jeroboam, existed from 937-722 B.C.E. It was destroyed by Assyria.
see chart, p. 72

ISRAEL, STATE OF
In 1948 the new State of Israel was founded. It extends from the Mediterranean to the Jordan and the Dead Sea, from the Lebanon to Elath. Parts of ancient Israel now belong to Jordan and Lebanon. The remains of the Temple (the Wailing Wall), Hebron and the Cave of Machpelah, where the Patriarchs were buried, are all in Arab hands. The creation of the new State marks the first time Jews have been independent in their ancient land since the destruction of the Second Temple in 70 C.E.

ISSACHAR
Ninth son of Jacob, fifth son of Leah, ancestor of the tribe of Issachar.

ISSACHAR, TRIBE OF
One of the tribes of Israel. Its territory was the fertile eastern section of the Emek Jezreel and the northern hills, near the tribe of Zebulun. Issachar's emblem was a donkey; its black banner depicted the sun and the moon. The stone representing Issachar in the high priest's breastplate was probably a sapphire.

IVRIT
see Hebrew

IYAR
Eighth month in the Jewish calendar.
see Months, Jewish

JABBOK

The great river of ancient Gilead which flows into the eastern bank of the Jordan. Jacob, on his return from Haran, wrestled with the angel on the bank of the Jabbok, where he was named Israel.

(Genesis, chap. 32: 23-33)

JABESH-GILEAD

Town east of the Jordan, in Gilead, saved by King Saul, in his first battle, from its enemies, the Ammonites. At the time of Saul's tragic death in the battle of Gilboa, the brave men of Jabesh-gilead saved the bodies of Saul and his sons from the Philistines and buried them in Jabesh-gilead.

(Samuel I, chap. 11; chap. 31: 8-13)

JABIN

Canaanite king whose general, Sisera, was defeated by Deborah and Barak in a battle at Mount Tabor.

(Judges, chap. 4)

JACOB

Third of the Patriarchs, son of Isaac and Rebekah, brother of Esau from whom he took his birthright, husband of Leah and Rachel, father of 12 sons who became the ancestors of the 12 tribes of Israel. Jacob's name was changed to Israel *(he who wrestled with God)* when he wrestled with the angel on his return from Haran to Canaan. In his old age he migrated to Egypt with his family where he was reunited with his son Joseph. Jacob was buried in the Cave of Machpelah.

JACOB BEN ASHER

see Turim

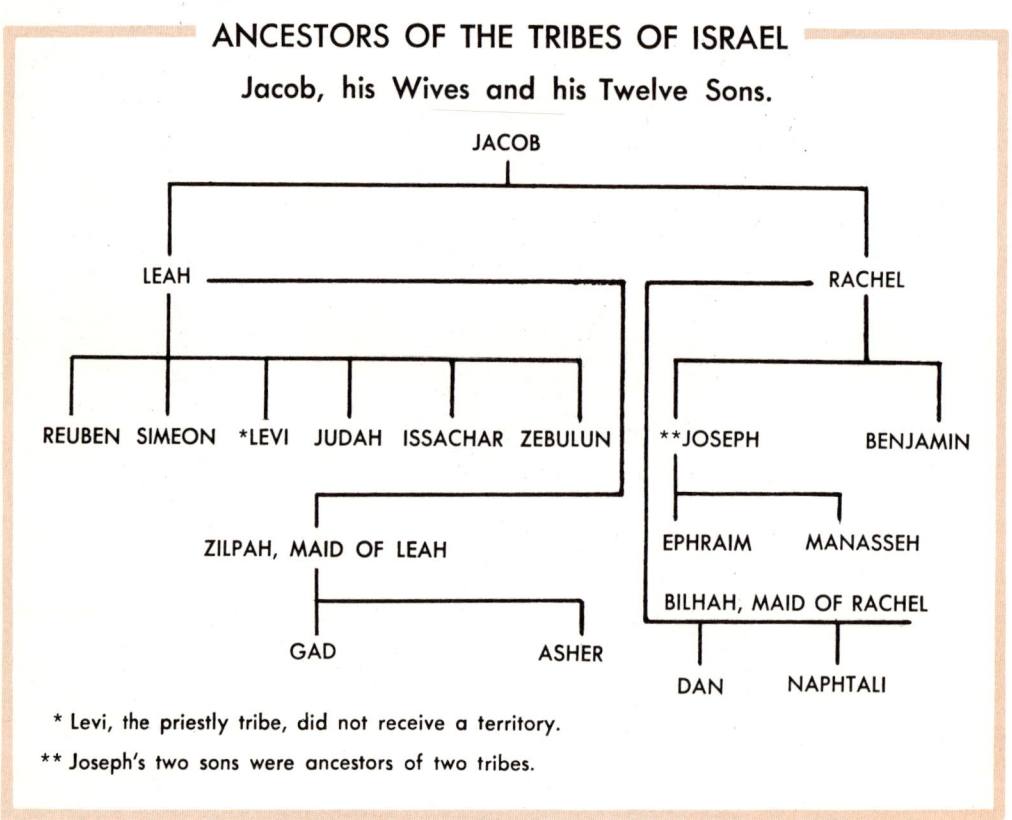

ANCESTORS OF THE TRIBES OF ISRAEL
Jacob, his Wives and his Twelve Sons.

* Levi, the priestly tribe, did not receive a territory.
** Joseph's two sons were ancestors of two tribes.

JACOB BEN MEIR
see Tosafot

JAEL
Heroic Kenite woman who slew Sisera, general of the Canaanites, on his flight from the victorious Barak.
(Judges, chap. 4: 17-23)

JAIR
Of Gilead, Judge of Israel who defeated the Ammonites and judged for twenty-two years.
(Judges, chap. 10: 3-5)

JAPHET
One of Noah's three sons. According to Biblical tradition, he is the ancestor of the Indo-European peoples.

JAVNEH, ACADEMY OF
Talmudic academy in Javneh, founded by Johanan Ben Zakkai at the time of the destruction of the Second Temple. In the middle of the 2nd century, during Bar Kochba's revolt, Javneh was destroyed by the Romans. The scholars fled and moved their academy to Usha. In Judah Hanasi's time it moved again, to Sepphoris, and it also met at Tiberias and Bet-Shearim. The scholars of Javneh made great contributions to the Mishnah.

JEBUSITES
Strong tribe hostile to the Israelites during the time of Saul and David. David and his general, Joab, captured the fortified city of Jerusalem from the Jebusites.
(Samuel II, chap. 5:6-10)

JECONIAH
see Jehoiachin

JEHOAHAZ
1. Also called Shallum, seventeenth king of Judah, son of Josiah. After a reign of three months, he was taken captive by Pharaoh Necoh and died in Egypt, in 608 B.C.E.
(Kings II, chap. 23: 31-34)
2. Eleventh king of Israel, son of Jehu (ruled about 815-798 B.C.E.). During his reign the rulers of Damascus threatened Israel, but their defeat by the Assyrians removed this threat.
(Kings II, chap. 13: 1-9)

JEHOASH
Twelfth king of Israel (about 798-782 B.C.E.), son of Jehoahaz, warred successfully against Aram and battled with Judah.
(Kings II, chap. 13: 10; chap. 14: 16)

JEHOIACHIN
Also called Jeconiah, nineteenth and next to the last king of Judah (about 597 B.C.E.) before the Babylonian

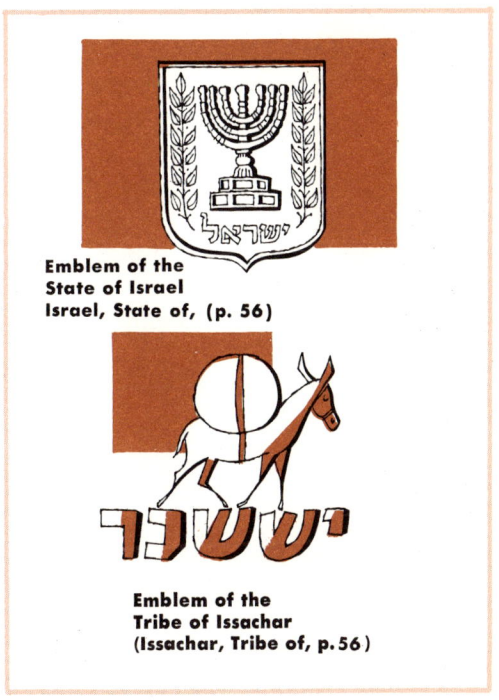

Emblem of the State of Israel
Israel, State of, (p. 56)

Emblem of the Tribe of Issachar
(Issachar, Tribe of, p. 56)

Exile, son of King Jehoiakim. He was imprisoned by Nebuchadnezzar and, together with his family and many important citizens, deported to Babylon.

(Kings II, chap. 24: 8-17)

JEHOIADA
Faithful priest who helped save Prince Joash from his scheming grandmother, Athaliah, and later helped put Joash on the throne of Judah.

(Kings II, chap. 11)

JEHOIAKIM
Also called Eliakim, eighteenth king of Judah (about 608-597 B.C.E.), second son of King Josiah, succeeded his brother Jehoahaz. Jehoiakim was an irreverent king. He ignored the warnings and prophecies of Jeremiah. In his 11-year rule the yoke of Egypt was replaced by that of Babylon. Jehoiakim led the revolt against Babylonia that resulted in the destruction of Jerusalem and the Temple.

(Kings II, chap. 23: 34-chap. 24: 5)

JEHORAM (JORAM)
1. Ninth king of Israel (about 852-842 B.C.E.), son of Ahab and Jezebel, successor to his older brother Ahaziah. Jehoram continued his parents' cruelties and worshipped the idol Baal. Jehu, an officer in his army, revolted and slew him. Jehu succeeded Jehoram.

(Kings II, chaps. 3 and 9)

2. Son of Jehoshaphat; fifth king of Judah (about 851-843 B.C.E.), married Athaliah, daughter of Ahab and Jezebel. He was an unpopular king. Influenced by the House of Ahab, he encouraged worship of Baal. He died of a painful disease, as predicted by the prophet Elijah.

(Kings II, chap. 8: 16-24)

JEHOSHAPHAT
Fourth king of Judah (about 876-851 B.C.E.), ruled at the time of King Ahab of Israel. He fought idolatry, sending priests and Levites to teach the people of Judah their religion. Judah flourished under his reign.

(Kings I, chap. 22)

JEHOSHEBA
Daughter of King Jehoram of Judah, aunt of Prince Joash whom she and her husband, the high priest Jehoiadah, hid from the scheming Queen Athaliah.

(Kings II, chap. 11)

JEHU
Tenth king of Israel (about 842-815 B.C.E.). He slew the idolatrous Queen Jezebel and rid Israel of the House of Ahab and Baal's priests. Anointed by the prophet Elisha, who had a great influence on him, he was the first king of Israel to forbid idol worship.

(Kings II, chaps. 9-10)

JEPHTHAH
Great Judge in Israel. He drove the invading Ammonites out of Gilead and became the leader of the Gileadites. Later he led the men of Ephraim to victory over the Ammonites. He helped unite and strengthen the tribes of Israel.

(Judges, chaps. 11-12: 7)

JEREMIAH
Second of the three Major Prophets. His words are recorded in the Biblical Book of Jeremiah. He was active from the reign of King Josiah to that of King Zedekiah, at the time of the destruction of Judah. Jeremiah opposed war and advised Zedekiah not to revolt against Babylonia, in order to save Jerusalem from destruction. But his advice was not heeded. When

the city was destroyed and Judah fell, Jeremiah gave comfort and hope to the people and prophesied the rebuilding of Jerusalem. After the assassination of his friend, the governor Gedaliah, Jeremiah was forced into exile to Egypt where he died.

JEREMIAH, BOOK OF

Second of the Books of the three Major Prophets of the Bible. It contains the words of the prophet Jeremiah.

JEREMIAH, EPISTLE OF

Sixth chapter of the Book of Baruch, part of the Apocrypha. Baruch was the loyal disciple of Jeremiah.

JERICHO

Ancient fortified city in the Jordan valley near Jerusalem. In the Book of Joshua it is told how the walls of Jericho crumbled under the blowing of the Israelites' mighty trumpets. Jericho has been excavated in modern times.

(Joshua, chap. 6)

JEROBOAM

First king of the northern Kingdom of Israel (about 937-915 B.C.E.). He had revolted against King Solomon and fled to Egypt. During the reign of arrogant Rehoboam he returned. When the kingdom split into two, he led the rebellious northern tribes in establishing the Kingdom of Israel and became its king.

(Kings I, chap. 11:26-chap. 14:20)

JEROBOAM II

Great grandson of Jehu; thirteenth king of Israel (about 782-741 B.C.E.), at the time of the prophet Amos. Amos criticized Jeroboam's prosperous reign because of the great differences between the rich and the poor of the kingdom. Amos also warned Jeroboam against the mighty Assyrians.

(Kings II, chap. 14: 23-29)

JERUBBAAL

see Gideon

JERUSALEM

Beautiful, ancient city, the religious and political center of Israel and Judah. Taken by David from the Jebusites, he made it his capital and brought the Ark there. Solomon's Temple and the Second Temple stood in Jerusalem. It was the center of Jewish life until the destruction of the Temple in 70 C.E. After Bar Kochba's revolt (about 135 C.E.), Hadrian forbade Jews to live there. Today, only part of Jerusalem is in Israel; one part, including the Temple area, is in Jordan.

JESHURUN

Poetic name for Israel, meaning "courageous one," or "righteous one."

JESSE

Prosperous farmer of Bethlehem, father of David, descendant of Ruth and Boaz.

JETHRO

The noble Kenite priest of Midian; father-in-law of Moses who found refuge with Jethro after he fled from Egypt. Jethro accompanied Moses during the wanderings in the wilderness. He helped install the first judges of Israel to assist Moses in his difficult tasks.

(Exodus, chap. 2: 15-22; chap. 18)

JEW

(*Yehudi*) originally the name for a member of the tribe of Judah. After the return from Babylonian Exile, the name for all Israelites became Jews (*Yehudim*).

JEWISH WAR

see Josephus Flavius

JEZEBEL

Queen, wife of King Ahab of Israel, Phoenician princess from Tyre. She sought to replace Israel's religion with Baal. She encouraged Ahab in his injustices and cruelty. She persecuted the prophets. Elijah opposed her. His successor, the prophet Elisha, encouraged the revolt of Jehu against Jezebel and her son, Jehoram. Jezebel was slain by Jehu.

(Kings I, chap. 16: 31-33; chap. 19: 1-2; chap. 21; Kings II, chap. 9: 30-37)

JOAB

Capable and devoted general of King David. He was victorious in many battles and helped conquer Jerusalem, then a Jebusite fortress.

(Samuel II, chaps. 2-3, 10, 18-19)

JOASH

Eighth king of Judah (about 836-796 B.C.E.), son of Ahaziah, saved by Jehoiadah from his scheming grandmother, Queen Athaliah. When Joash was six years old, Jehoiadah called the nobles of Jerusalem and presented Joash, their rightful king. The nobles revolted against Queen Athaliah. Joash cleansed the Temple of idols, rid the country of Baal and put an end to the cruelties of Athaliah.

(Kings II, chaps. 11-12)

JOB, BOOK OF

Third book of the 3rd division (*Ketubim*) of the Bible. Job, a righteous man, was tested by God and was made to suffer great misfortunes. He withstood all the tests and preserved his faith.

JOCHEBED

Wife of Amram, of the tribe of Levi, mother of Moses, Aaron and Miriam.

(Exodus, chap. 2: 1-10; chap. 6: 20)

Jacob (p. 58)

Jerusalem (p. 61)

Jeremiah (p. 60)

JOEL

Second Book of the Twelve (Minor) Prophets of the Bible. He described with scientific accuracy a terrible plague of locusts that had taken place, and he drew moral lessons from this tragic experience.

JOHANAN

Son of Mattathias; brother of Judah Maccabee; one of the leaders in the revolt against Antiochus.

JOHANAN BAR NAPPAHA

Scholar and teacher, one of the founders of the Palestinian Talmud. Rabbi Johanan, a student of Judah Hanasi, headed his own school at Sepphoris, but, after a scholarly disagreement, left and joined the academy of Tiberias. There he met Simeon Ben Lakish. Impressed by the mind and personality of Simeon, he convinced him to join him and become a scholar. The famous discussions between Johanan and Simeon were recorded in the Talmud.

JOHANAN BEN ZAKKAI

Great Tannaitic scholar, helped preserve the traditions of Torah at the time of the destruction of the Temple, founder of the academy of Javneh, died about 80 C.E.. It is said that he let his students carry him out of besieged Jerusalem in a coffin, to enable him to seek permission from the Roman general, who later became Emperor Vespasian, to found the school at Javneh.

JONAH

Fifth of the Books of Twelve (Minor) Prophets of the Bible. It is a narrative (the other Later Prophetic writings are mainly orations) relating how Jonah, son of Amittai, of the tribe of Zebulun, avoided God's command to go to the Assyrian capital Nineveh and preach against its wickedness, by taking a sea voyage. During a storm, he was thrown overboard and was swallowed by a great whale who spewed him out near Nineveh, where Jonah fulfilled his mission. The book of Jonah is read on Yom Kippur.

JONATHAN

1. Noble warrior prince, son of King Saul, victor of many battles against the Philistines. Though his father bitterly turned on David, Jonathan remained David's loyal friend. Both Saul and Jonathan fell in the battle of Mount Gilboa. David wrote a beautiful song lamenting the deaths of Saul, his king, and of his friend, Jonathan.

(Samuel I, chaps. 14, 18-20, 31; Samuel II, chap. 1)

2. Son of Mattathias; brother of Judah Maccabee; military leader and high priest of Judea.

JORAM

see Jehoram

JORDAN

1. The beautiful major river of the land of Israel, scene of many important Biblical events. The Jordan takes its rise on the slopes of Mount Hermon, flows through the Sea of Galilee and ends in the Dead Sea. The Israelites' crossing of the Jordan to the Promised Land is described in the Book of Joshua.

2. The Kingdom of Jordan, established in 1946, consists of most of the ancient territories of Gilead, Moab and Edom. Part of Jerusalem is in Jordan.

JOSEPH

Eleventh son of Jacob; first son of Rachel, father of Ephraim and Manasseh. Joseph was sold by his jealous brothers into Egyptian slavery. In Egypt his ability to interpret dreams led him to become second in command to Pharaoh. Through his wisdom Egypt was saved from famine. He was reunited with his father and brothers when they came to Egypt to escape the famine. Joseph, one of the most beloved Biblical figures, has inspired artists and writers throughout the ages.

(Genesis, chaps. 37-50)

JOSEPHUS FLAVIUS (JOSEPH BEN MATTATHIAS)

Historian, unsuccessful defender of Galilee in the Jewish War (66-67 C.E.) who gave himself up to the Romans. Josephus had a colorful career. He was first honored and trusted, but later was accused of inefficiency, cowardice and even treachery. After the fall of the fortress Jotapata, he and a companion were the only surviving Jewish soldiers. Josephus went to Rome and took the family name Flavius of his benefactor, Emperor Vespasian. In Rome he wrote "Antiquities" and "The Jewish War."

JOSHUA

1. Son of Nun, of the tribe of Ephraim, Moses' assistant and general, who, after Moses' death, led the Israelites into Canaan. He conquered Jericho and nearly the entire land of Canaan and helped the Israelites settle in their new land. He staunchly upheld the Israelites' religion against the new influences of Canaan. With the high priest Phinehas, he established the sanctuary of the Ark in Shiloh.

2. Ben Jehozadak, first high priest of the Second Temple, helped Zerubbabel rebuild the Temple and restore the Jewish community.

(Ezra, chap. 3)

Joseph being sold by his brothers (Joseph, p. 64)

Joshua (p. 64)

JOSHUA, BOOK OF

First Book of the Early Prophets (*Nevi'im Rishonim*) of the Bible. It records Israel's history from after the death of Moses to the conquest and settling of Canaan, under Joshua's leadership.

JOSIAH

Sixteenth king of Judah (about 639-608 B.C.E.), cleansed the Temple of idols and destroyed Baal's altar at Bethel. A lost scroll of the Torah was found in the Temple, book of Deuteronomy. Josiah, aided by Huldah, the prophetess, and Hilkiah, the high priest, read it to the people and helped restore their faith. At the end of his reign King Josiah courageously attempted to halt the advancing Egyptians. He was slain by Pharaoh Necoh of Egypt, at Megiddo (about 608 B.C.E.).

(Kings II, chaps. 22-23: 30)

JOTAPATA

see Josephus

JOTHAM

Eleventh king of Judah (about 737-735 B.C.E.), son of Uzziah, became ruler when aging Uzziah was stricken with leprosy. He continued to fortify Judah as his father had done. He lived at the time of the prophets Micah, Hosea and Isaiah.

(Kings II, chap. 15: 32-38)

JUBILEE, YEAR OF

A sacred year proclaimed every fifty years. In this year all land was returned to the original owners or their descendants, all slaves were freed, and no agriculture was permitted.

(Leviticus, chap. 25: 1-18)

JUDAH

Fourth son of Jacob and Leah, ancestor of the tribe of Judah.

see Judah, Tribe of

JUDAH HALEVI

Great Jewish poet of the Middle Ages, born in Spain, about 1080, died in Palestine, about 1145. His best known works are "Songs of Zion" and "Al Khazari," a defense of Judaism, written in the form of a discussion between a Jewish scholar and a king of the Khazars who had converted to Judaism after examining many faiths. It is told that Judah Halevi, while on a pilgrimage to Jerusalem, died under the hoofs of a cruel Arab rider. He recited one of his Songs of Zion while he was dying.

Emblem of the Tribe of Judah (Judah, Tribe of, p. 67)

Jonah (p. 63)

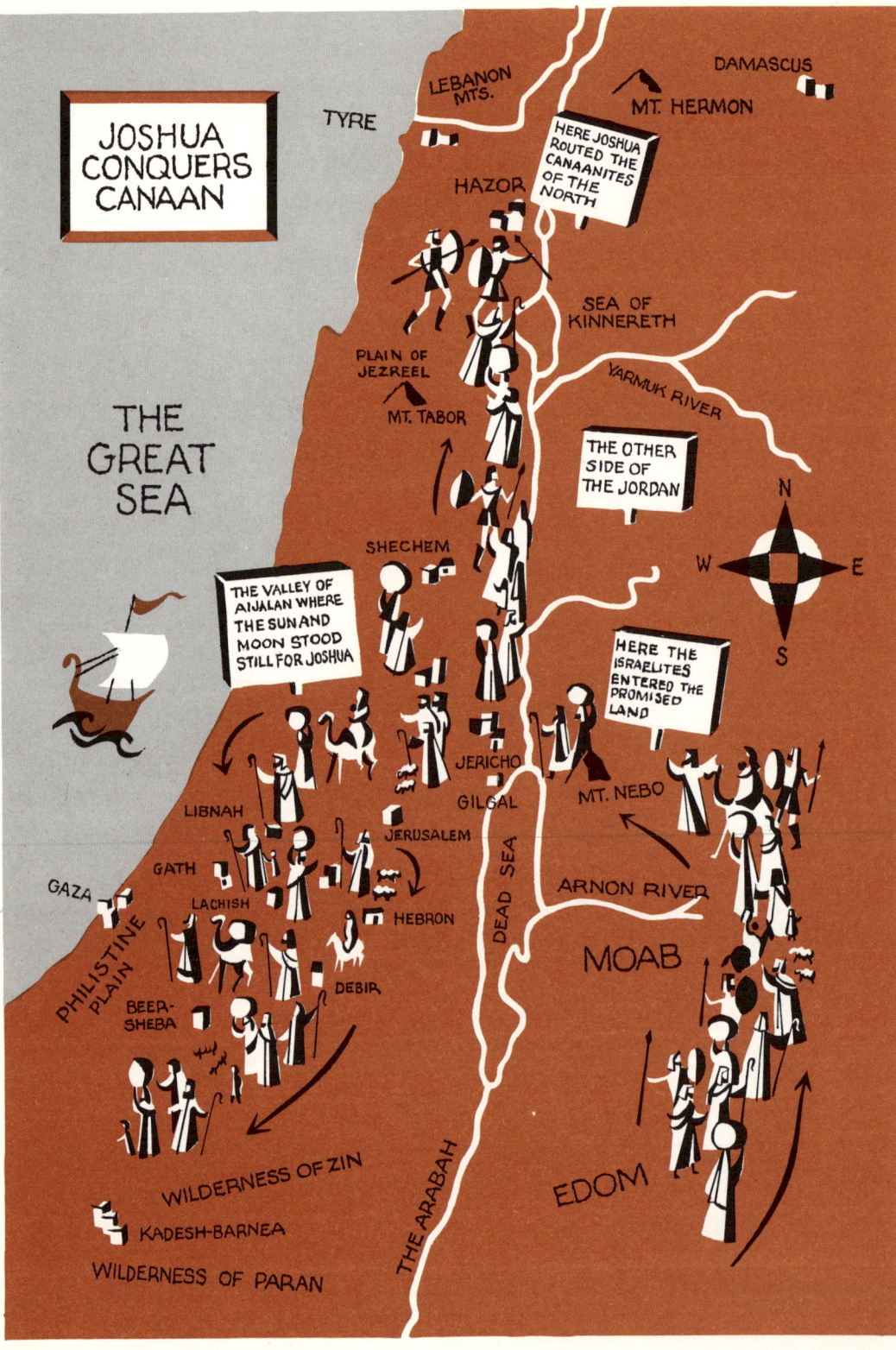

JUDAH HANASI

Brilliant compiler of the Mishnah, lived 135-200 C.E., succeeded his father, Simeon Ben Gamaliel II as Nasi; head of the academies of Tiberias, Bet-Shearim and Sepphoris. He was called Rabbi or Rabbenu Hakadosh (*our holy teacher*), because of his great learning, piety and unselfish charity. He was well versed in many subjects and languages. Though a wealthy man, Judah Hanasi lived simply, dedicated to his great task, the collecting and writing down of the Oral Torah—the Mishnah.

JUDAH, KINGDOM OF

(937-586 B.C.E.), founded after the rebellion of the northern tribes who established the Kingdom of Israel. Judah was ruled by the House of David. It consisted of the tribes of Judah and Benjamin. With the destruction of the First Temple and the Babylonian Exile, the Kingdom of Judah, under the House of David, ended. The history of the Kingdom of Judah is recorded in the two Books of Kings in the Bible.

see chart, p. 72

JUDAH MACCABEE

(*The hammer*) leader of the Maccabean revolt, one of the five brave sons of Mattathias. He led the Judeans to victory and rededicated the Temple Antiochus had desecrated.

JUDAH, TRIBE OF

One of the tribes of Israel. It occupied the greater southern part of Canaan. Judah's leadership among the tribes was established at the time of the Kings. David was of the tribe of Judah. At the time of the division of the kingdom, Judah gave the southern kingdom its name and became its center. Judah's banner was sky-blue; its emblem was a lion. The stone representing Judah in the breastplate of the high priest was probably an emerald.

JUDAISM

The name of the religion of the Jewish people, apparently first used in the 1st century C. E. by Greek-speaking Jews to describe their religion as distinct from the religion of their neighbors, Hellenism. As the centuries passed, the term Judaism was used by Jews and non-Jews alike to distinguish it from other religions. Orthodox Judaism, Conservative Judaism, Reform Judaism and Reconstructionism are comparatively new terms used to describe the various branches of American Judaism. In general, these groups all accept the basic ethical, moral and social principles of Judaism and draw their inspiration from the same Biblical and rabbinical writings. They differ on the place of the law in Judaism, particularly the laws dealing with rites and ceremonies.

1. Orthodox Judaism maintains strictly the traditional laws of the Bible as they were interpreted and developed by the early rabbis in the Talmud and other works of Jewish law (the Rabbinic tradition).

2. Conservative Judaism accepts the authority of Jewish ceremonial and ritual laws and believes that these laws strengthen the Jewish community socially and spiritually. But it has adopted a number of important modifications in practicing them to meet the new conditions of modern life.

3. Reform Judaism maintains that the laws of the Bible and the Talmudic tradition may be changed (reformed) or developed to meet the

needs of new situations, and that this process of development must continue. Reform Judaism has modified many rituals and observances.

4. Reconstructionism accepts from Orthodox Judaism the stress on a maximum of Jewish life and from Reform Judaism the concept of need for development. It maintains that it is important for the Jew to gain knowledge of Judaism and to participate meaningfully in Jewish life.

JUDEA

Name of the Second Commonwealth after the Babylonian Exile. Judea was bounded by Samaria on the north, Edom (Idumea) on the south, the Mediterranean on the west, and the Jordan and Dead Sea on the east. Judea was governed by priests and in its latter days ruled by kings of the Hasmonean and Herodian dynasties. Judea was independent only a short time, under the Hasmoneans (Maccabees). It became a vassal of Persia, Syria and later of Rome. It existed from approximately 539 B.C.E.-70 C.E.

see Hasmonean Dynasty
see Herodian Dynasty

JUDGES

(*Shofetim*) in ancient times judges were leaders who functioned only incidentally as judges in the modern sense. As leaders, they were often soldiers or priests or prophets. Twelve Judges are described in the Book of Judges. But other men who judged are mentioned in other parts of the Bible. The lives of the Judges Eli and Samuel are described in Samuel I.

JUDGES, BOOK OF

(*Shofetim*) second book of the Early Prophets (*Nevi'im Rishonim*) of the Bible. It records the period of the twelve Judges, Israel's history from

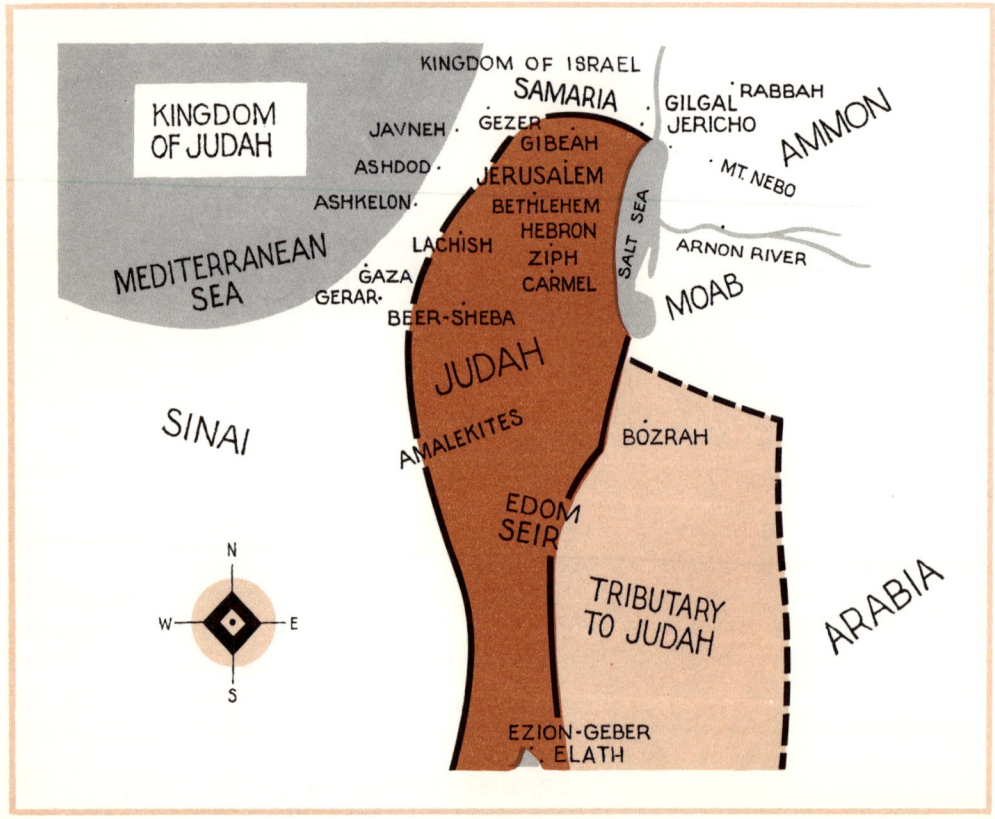

the time of the death of Joshua to that of the birth of Samuel.

JUDITH, BOOK OF
Book of the Apocrypha. It relates the story of Judith, the beautiful widow who saved the fortress Bethulia from destruction by killing the Assyrian general, Holofernes.

KABBALAH
see Cabala

KADDISH
(*Holy*) ancient prayer in Aramaic declaring and blessing the greatness and holiness of God, and asking for the coming of the Messiah and God's kingdom of peace. The Kaddish is said several times during services, and usually at the conclusion. The Kaddish is best known as the prayer in memory of the dead, recited by close relatives at the time of mourning and at Yiskor and Yahrzeit.

KADESH-BARNEA
Oasis in the Sinai desert, south of ancient Canaan, where Miriam was buried and from where Moses sent the first scouts to Canaan. Kadesh-barnea was a central camp site of the Israelites during their forty years of wanderings. It was the starting point for their final march to Canaan.

(Numbers, chaps. 13 and 20)

KALLAH
see Hatunah

KARAITES
Jewish sect, possibly developed out of the old sect (party) of the Sadducees. They rejected the rabbinic tradition, the Talmudic writings and commentaries on the laws of the Torah, and accepted only the Torah. But over the centuries the Karaites developed a tradition of writings just as binding for them as the rabbinic tradition. Karaites, now a small sect, have lived in the Middle East (many of their writings are in Arabic), the Caucasus area, Crimea, Poland and Lithuania.

KASHRUT
(*Fitness, worthiness*) refers generally to any object or person which meets all traditional Jewish requirements. Specifically it refers to foods which are considered kosher.

see Kosher

see Dietary Laws

KEDESH
City of Refuge in the territory of Naphtali.

see Cities of Refuge

KEDUSHAH
(*Sanctification*) a dramatic daily prayer that acknowledges the ma-

---

JUDGES

The Twelve Judges of Israel whose histories are told in the Book of Judges: *

OTHNIEL	DEBORAH	JAIR	ELON
EHUD	GIDEON	JEPHTHAH	ABDON
SHAMGAR	TOLA	IBZAN	SAMSON

* The lives of the later Judges, Eli and Samuel, are told in the Book of Samuel, I.

jesty and holiness of God. It is recited in the form of alternate chanting by the cantor or reader and the congregation. The Kedushah is based on the visions of Isaiah and Ezekiel.
(Isaiah, chap. 6: 1-4; Ezekiel, chap. 3: 12-14)

KENITES
Nomadic tribe which originally dwelt in the Sinai Desert, related to the Midianites. They were accomplished coppersmiths. Jethro, Moses' father-in-law, was a Kenite of Midian. Many Kenites went with the Israelites to Canaan.

KERIAH
The ancient custom of rending a garment as an expression of grief over the death of a close relative. Today orthodox Jews observe a moderate form of Keriah *(rending)*.

KERIAT HATORAH
The "Reading of the Torah" during the synagogue services.

KERIAT SHEMA
Also called Krishma, the reading of the Shema which occurs in the morning and evening prayers and before retiring.

see Shema

KETER TORAH
(*Crown of the Torah*) made of silver, part of the ornamentation of the Torah.

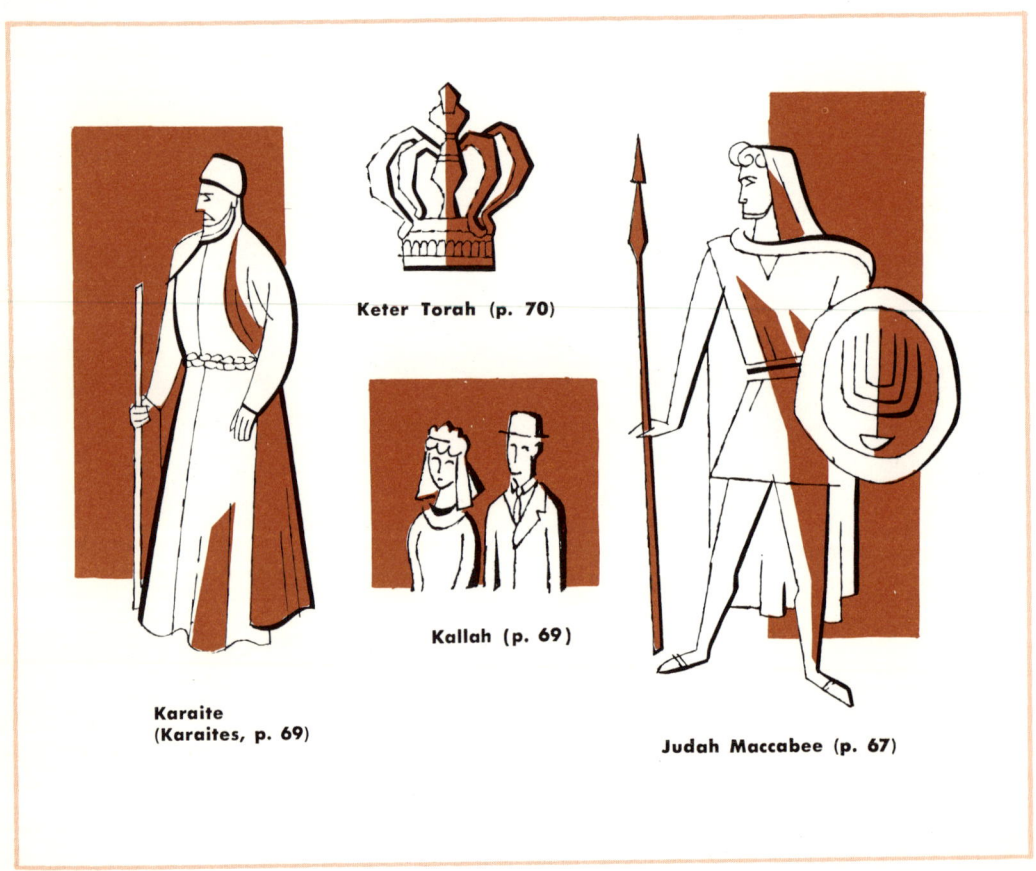

Keter Torah (p. 70)

Kallah (p. 69)

Karaite (Karaites, p. 69)

Judah Maccabee (p. 67)

KETIVAH TOVAH

A greeting used on Rosh Hashanah, meaning "may you be written down well." It refers to the belief that on the New Year each man's fate for the coming year is written down by God into the Book of Life.

KETUBAH

The written document of the marriage contract which lists the obligations of the groom.

KETUBIM

(*Writings*) the third and last division of the Bible. Ketubim contains eleven books, arranged in three parts. The first part, the three poetical books, or Sifre Emet (*Books of Truth*), contains: Psalms, Proverbs and Job. The second part, the Five Megillot (*Scrolls*), contains: Song of Songs, Ruth, Lamentations, Ecclesiastes and Esther. The third part, the historical writings, contains: Daniel, Ezra-Nehemiah, and Chronicles I and II. The Greek name for Ketubim is Hagiographa (*sacred writings*).

KETUBIM AHARONIM

see Apocrypha.

KHAZARS

Medieval people of southern Russia whose kings and nobles converted to Judaism in the eighth century.
see Judah Halevi

KIDDUSH

(*Sanctification*) a blessing recited over a cup of wine at the beginning of every Sabbath and holiday. Kiddush in the synagogue is said at the end of Friday evening service (*Maariv*). Since ancient times, Kiddush is best known as a home ceremony, said by the man of the household, ushering in the Sabbath at the beginning of the Friday evening meal.

KIDDUSH CUP

The special cup for the wine to be blessed at the Kiddush ceremony either in the synagogue or at home. Kiddush cups are usually made of silver and often beautifully decorated.

KINGS I AND II, BOOKS OF

Fourth and last book of the Early Prophets (*Nevi'im Rishonim*) of the Bible. The two sections of the book recount four centuries of Jewish history. They begin with the last days of King David (about 977 B.C.E.) and conclude with the destruction of the First Temple, the Babylonian Exile and the release of Jehoiachin from Babylonian prison.

KINGS OF ISRAEL AND JUDAH

see chart, p. 72
see Israel, Kingdom of
see Judah, Kingdom of

KINOT

(*Lamentations*) a special service observed in the synagogue on Tisha B'Av, in commemoration of the destruction of the Temples, during which the Book of Lamentations is read.

KIPPAH

see Skullcap

KIRIATH-JEARIM

(*Town of Forests*) a town on the border of Judah and Benjamin. After the Philistines had captured the Ark, they abandoned it at Kiriath-jearim. There priests watched over it until David took it to Jerusalem.

(Samuel I, chap. 6:20-chap. 7:4)

KINGS OF ISRAEL AND JUDAH

KINGS BEFORE DIVISION OF KINGDOM

1040–1017 B.C.E. SAUL
1010–977 B.C.E. DAVID
977–937 B.C.E. SOLOMON

ISH-BOSHETH
about 1017–1010 B.C.E.
(ruled only over part of Israel)

THE NORTHERN KINGDOM OF ISRAEL

THE KINGDOM OF JUDAH

ruled by the House of David

937–722 B.C.E.

937–915 B.C.E.	1. JEROBOAM
915–914 B.C.E.	2. NADAB
914–890 B.C.E.	3. BAASA (BAASHA)
890–889 B.C.E.	4. ELAH
889 B.C.E.	5. ZIMRI
889–875 B.C.E.	6. OMRI
875–853 B.C.E.	7. AHAB
853–852 B.C.E.	8. AHAZIAH
852–842 B.C.E.	9. JEHORAM (JORAM)
842–815 B.C.E.	10. JEHU
815–798 B.C.E.	11. JEHOAHAZ
798–782 B.C.E.	12. JEHOASH
782–741 B.C.E.	13. JEROBOAM II
741 B.C.E.	14. ZECHARIAH
741 B.C.E.	15. SHALLUM
741–737 B.C.E.	16. MENAHEM
737–736 B.C.E.	17. PEKAHIAH
736–734 B.C.E.	18. PEKAH
734–722 B.C.E.	19. HOSHEA

722 B.C.E. The Assyrians destroy Samaria and lead the Ten Tribes, the people of Israel, into captivity.

937–586 B.C.E.

937–920 B.C.E.	1. REHOBOAM
920–917 B.C.E.	2. ABIJAH (ABIJAM)
917–876 B.C.E.	3. ASA
876–851 B.C.E.	4. JEHOSHAPHAT
851–843 B.C.E.	5. JEHORAM (JORAM)
843–842 B.C.E.	6. AHAZIAH
842–836 B.C.E.	7. ATHALIAH (WIFE OF JEHORAM)
836–796 B.C.E.	8. JOASH
796–767 B.C.E.	9. AMAZIAH
767–737 B.C.E.	10. UZZIAH (AZARIAH)
737–735 B.C.E.	11. JOTHAM
735–720 B.C.E.	12. AHAZ
720–692 B.C.E.	13. HEZEKIAH
692–641 B.C.E.	14. MANASSEH
641–639 B.C.E.	15. AMON
639–608 B.C.E.	16. JOSIAH
608 B.C.E.	17. JEHOAHAZ (Shallum)
608–597 B.C.E.	18. JEHOIAKIM (ELIAKIM)
597 B.C.E.	19. JEHOIACHIN (JECONIAH)
597–586 B.C.E.	20. ZEDEKIAH (MATTANIAH)

586 B.C.E. End of the Kingdom of Judah. The Babylonian Exile.

All dates are approximate

Red signifies the start of a new dynasty

KISHON, RIVER

Small river north of Mount Carmel and near Mount Tabor. During the rainy season it sometimes swells to a torrential stream. A sudden storm that increased the Kishon's power was an important factor in the defeat of Sisera, as described in Deborah's Song. The prophet Elijah slew Baal's priests near this river.

KISLEV

Third month in the Jewish calendar.

see Months, Jewish

KITZUR SHULHAN ARUKH

Shortened popular edition of the Shulhan Arukh, widely used as a handbook on Jewish law by Orthodox Jews.

see Shulhan Arukh

KODASHIM

see Sedarim

KOHELET

see Ecclesiastes, Book of

KOL NIDRE

(*All vows*) a prayer chanted by the cantor at the beginning of the synagogue service on Yom Kippur eve. The prayer asks God for forgiveness for all vows that will be made to Him (concerning only oneself and not one's fellowmen) and that will not be kept. The Kol Nidre is chanted to an ancient beautiful melody, and it serves as the name for the entire Yom Kippur eve service.

KORAH

A Levite who, with Dathan and Abiram, led an unsuccessful revolt against Moses and Aaron. The three were destroyed by an earthquake.

(Numbers, chap. 16)

KOSHER

(*Proper* or *prepared*) refers to food prepared in accordance with Jewish law and practice, also used to designate the animals (and their flesh) which are cloven-footed and chew the cud, and fish that have both fins and scales.

(Leviticus, chap. 11)

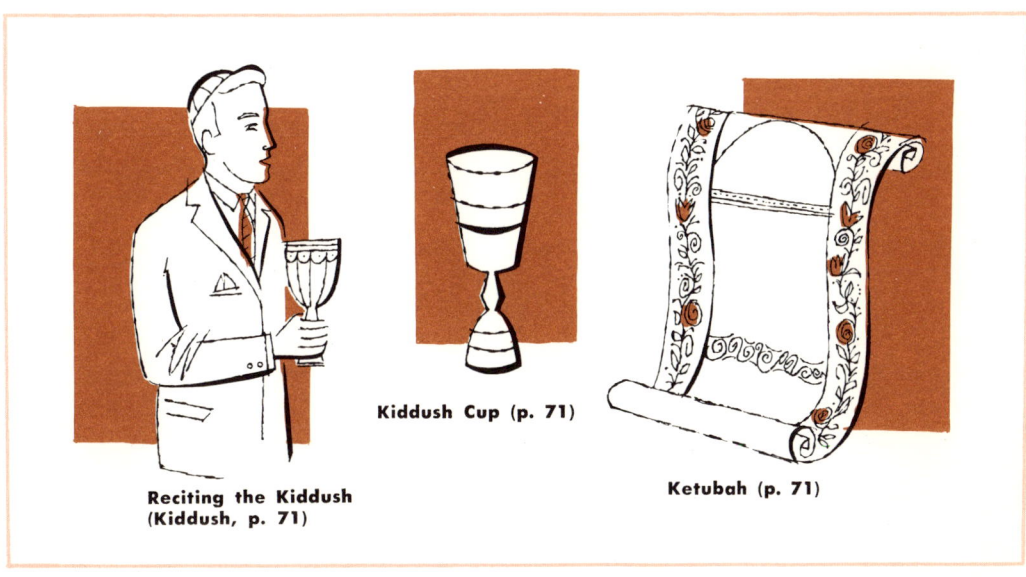

Reciting the Kiddush
(Kiddush, p. 71)

Kiddush Cup (p. 71)

Ketubah (p. 71)

KRISHMA
see Keriat Shema

LABAN
Brother of Rebekah, wealthy sheep and cattle breeder of Haran who gave work and refuge to his nephew Jacob. He was the father of Jacob's two wives, Leah and Rachel.
(Genesis, chaps. 29-32: 3)

LACHISH
Ancient fortress between Jerusalem and Gaza overlooking the main road connecting Egypt and the land of Israel. It was conquered by Joshua in one of his greatest victories. Later Lachish was taken by Nebuchadnezzar. It became the strong southern frontier fortress of the Persians during their rule of Judea. It has been excavated in modern times.
(Joshua, chap. 10: 31-33)

LADINO
Judeo-Spanish dialect spoken by Sephardim. Many beautiful religious writings and prayerbooks, literary works and songs have been written in Ladino.

LAG B'OMER
A half-holiday that observes the thirty-third day of the period of 49 days of Omer or Sefirah, between Passover and Shavuot, known as the "counting of Omer." It is also called the "Scholar's Festival" for it commemorates the struggle of Rabbi Akiba and his disciple, Simeon Bar Yohai, for freedom to study and observe God's law at the time of the oppression of the Jews by the Roman Emperor Hadrian.

LAMENTATIONS, BOOK OF
(Ekhah) third of the Five Megillot of the Bible. It contains songs of sorrow (elegies), ascribed to the prophet Jeremiah, mourning the destruction of Jerusalem and the Temple. Lamentations are chanted on Tisha B'Av (9th of Av), the day commemorating that event.

LEAH
Wife of Jacob, older sister of Rachel, daughter of Laban. Laban tricked Jacob into marrying her instead of Rachel. Leah was the mother of Ruben, Simeon, Levi, Judah, Zebulun, Issachar and Dinah. She was buried in the Cave of Machpelah. Leah is one of the Four Mothers of Israel.
(Genesis, chaps. 29-30: 21)

LEAVEN
see Hametz

LEBANON
1. Two beautiful mountain ranges, called the Lebanon and Anti-Lebanon, named for their snow-capped peaks. The Lebanon's highest peak is 10,200 feet high. The cedars and cypresses of Lebanon were famous for their beauty. King Solomon built the Temple with wood from the cedars of Lebanon.

2. The new republic at the northern border of the State of Israel (between Syria and the Mediterranean). Lebanon was established in 1942.

LECHAH DODI
Beautiful song welcoming the Sabbath. The author, Solomon Halevi Alkabetz (1540), calls Sabbath the beautiful bride.

LE-HAYIM
A toast, wishing life and health.

LE-SHANAH TOVAH

Greeting used during Rosh Hashanah and the Ten Days of Penitence. It means "a happy New Year."

LESHON HAKODESH

see Hebrew

LEVI

Third son of Jacob and Leah, ancestor of the tribe of Levi, the Levites and the Cohanim.

LEVITES

Members of the tribe of Levi, served in the Tabernacle and later in the Temple as assistants to the Cohanim. Levites were in charge of sacrifices, the rites of cleanliness and the guarding of the Temple. They also provided the sacred music. Today, the Levites still receive special honors in the synagogue service, second after the Cohanim.

LEVI, TRIBE OF

One of the tribes of Israel. The tribe of Levi, dedicated to temple service and the education of the people, received no portion of land in Israel—its portion was the Torah. Levi's banner was white, black and red; its emblem was the Urim and Tummim (priestly equipment). The stone representing Levi in the high priest's breastplate was probably a garnet.

LEVITICUS, BOOK OF

(*Vayikra*) third of the Biblical Five Books of Moses (the Torah). In Leviticus are found the priestly laws, the holiness and cleanliness code, and the laws of Yom Kippur. Leviticus also describes the installation of Israel's first priests (Aaron and his sons). Its 27 chapters are divided into 10 portions for weekly Sabbath readings.

LOST TRIBES OF ISRAEL

The tribes of the northern Kingdom of Israel which were deported and scattered by the Assyrian conquerors. Many people have speculated as to the present whereabouts and identity of the Lost Tribes. False claims have been made and many legends have grown around them throughout the centuries. No scholar to this day is certain what has become of them.

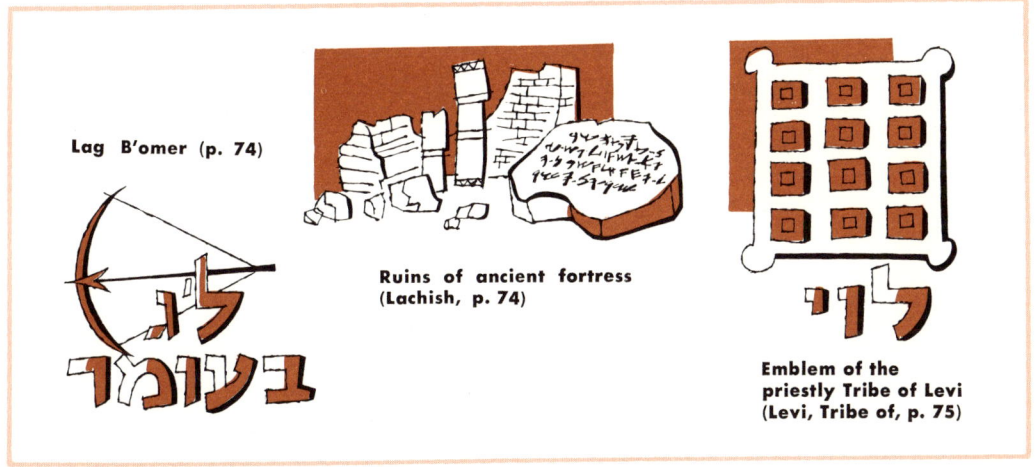

Lag B'omer (p. 74)

Ruins of ancient fortress (Lachish, p. 74)

Emblem of the priestly Tribe of Levi (Levi, Tribe of, p. 75)

LOT

Nephew of Abraham, son of Haran, from Ur. He accompanied Abraham to Canaan. He and his family lived in Sodom and were the only ones saved when the city was destroyed. His wife, however, who looked back at Sodom despite the angel's command, was turned into a pillar of salt.

(Genesis, chaps. 13 and 19)

LUACH

(*Tablet*) Hebrew word for calendar.

see Calendar, Jewish

LUCHOT HA B'RIT

see Tables of the Law

LULAV

A palm branch, one of the four plants used in the celebration of Sukkot. During the synagogue service, the branch is waved in all directions to show that God is to be found everywhere.

(Lev., chap. 23:40)

see Sukkot, Four Plants of

LURIA, ISAAC BEN SOLOMON

Great mystic scholar and teacher, founder of the Lurian Cabalist school at Safed. Many works of Cabala are ascribed to him, and his life has given rise to many beautiful Cabalist legends. He was born in Jerusalem in 1534 and died in Safed in 1572. In his short lifetime he exercised a great influence on Jewish mysticism.

LYDDA

City southeast of Jaffa; important center of Jewish revolt in Roman times. After the destruction of the Temple, Lydda was a refuge for scholars and became a seat of Jewish learning. An academy of Tannaim was established there.

MAARIV

The Evening Service, first of the three daily services (in the Jewish calendar, the day begins after sunset). The prayers of Maariv are recited after sunset.

MACCABEES

Five sons of the Hasmonean priest Mattathias, heroes of the Maccabean victory over Antiochus. The five Maccabees were Johanan, Simon, Eleazar, Jonathan and Judah Maccabee (*the Hammer*), from whom their name originated. The name Maccabee is also applied to the whole Hasmonean house and dynasty.

MACCABEES I and II

Books of the Apocrypha, a record of the religious thought, historical events and legends of the time of the Maccabees.

MACHPELAH

The cave and field near Hebron which Abraham bought from the Hittite, Ephron, for the burial of Sarah. The cave became the burial place for all the Patriarchs and for Rebekah and Leah. It is now in Arab territory, a sacred sanctuary of the Moslems who also consider Abraham their ancestor.

(Genesis, chap. 23)

MAFTIR

(*Conclusion*) originally the term referred to the person who concludes the portion of the Torah read in the synagogue on the Sabbath and holidays and who recites the reading from the Prophets (the Haftarah). It has now been extended to refer to the concluding Torah portion itself.

MAGEN DAVID

see Shield of David

MAGGID

(*Preacher*) in earlier times the rabbi seldom preached. This gap was filled by the Maggid, popular preacher who usually was not attached to a specific synagogue but went from place to place to deliver sermons.

MAH NISHTANAH

The opening words of the "Four Questions" asked by the youngest member of the family at the Passover Seder service. The "Four Questions" query the differences between the Passover night and other nights. "Why do we eat matzah? Why do we eat herbs? Why do we dip in salt water? Why do we recline instead of sitting erect?"

MAHZOR

(*Repetition* or *cycle of the year*) prayer book for the High Holy Days and the Three Festivals, containing the prayers, poetry and passages from the Scriptures to be recited on those days.

MAIMONIDES

Greatest Jewish philosopher and codifier of medieval times, often called RaMBaM from his title of rabbi and the initials of his name (Rabbi Moses ben Maimon), one of the leaders of the Jewish communities of his day, eminent physician to the Sultan of Egypt. He was born in Cordova, Spain, 1135,; died in Fostat (Old Cairo), Egypt, 1204. He was buried in Tiberias. His family fled from Islamic persecution in Spain and found refuge in Fostat. Maimonides wrote in Arabic and Hebrew. His many great works include Mishneh Torah, his brilliantly arranged code of Jewish law; Moreh Nevuchim (*Guide for the Perplexed*), his great philosophic work; and a commentary on the Mishnah which contains his well-known 13 Articles of Faith.

MAJOR PROPHETS

see Prophets, Major

MALACH

see Angel

MALACHI

Last of the Books of Twelve (Minor) Prophets of the Bible. Malachi (his real name is uncertain), a prophet of the fourth century B.C.E., talked against the evils of his time and proclaimed that all men are brothers, children of the One God, and that men should deal justly with one another.

MAMRE

1. Dwelling place of the Patriarchs, Abraham, Isaac and Jacob, either identical with Hebron or very near it. Abraham built an altar there.
(Genesis, chap. 13: 18)
2. Abraham's ally who helped him rescue Lot when the Canaanite kings had taken him prisoner.
(Genesis, chap. 14: 13 and 24)

MANASSEH

1. Older son of Joseph; grandson of Jacob, ancestor of the tribe of Manasseh.

2. Fourteenth king of Judah, son of Hezekiah, ruled about 692-641 B.C.E. Under his early rule idol worship flourished in Judah. Though he freely submitted Judah to Assyrian rule, he was temporarily taken captive to

Babylon. On his return, he upheld the religion of the One God.

(Kings II, chap. 21: 1-18;
Chron. II, chap. 33: 1-20)

MANASSEH, PRAYER OF

Book of the Apocrypha, a poem of penitence written in captivity, ascribed to King Manasseh of Judah.

MANASSEH, TRIBE OF

One of the tribes of Israel. It first settled in the north of Canaan, east of the Jordan. Later it joined its brother tribe, Ephraim, in the central region of Canaan. They shared the jet-black banner. Manasseh's emblem was a unicorn. The stone representing (Ephraim and) Manasseh in the high priest's breastplate was probably an onyx.

MANNA

Food from heaven that miraculously fell with the dew of the night near the camps of the Israelites during their wanderings in the barren wilderness. Manna is described as being similar to the manna of the tamarisk tree, still found in the Sinai Desert.

(Exodus, chap. 16;
Numbers, chap. 11: 7-9)

MANTLE

see Mappah

MAOZ TZUR

(*Rock of Ages*) a song sung at Hanukkah; the melody dates back to a German song of the 16th century.

MAPPAH

1. Decorative cover or mantle for the Torah, consisting of a headpiece, with two openings for the rollers of the Torah, and the covering piece itself.

2. Name of a code of law arranged by Moses Isserles, Ashkenazic scholar, published in Krakau, 1578. Mappah (*Tablecloth*) is a supplement to the Shulhan Arukh (*the Prepared Table*), the code of law arranged by Joseph Caro, in Safed.

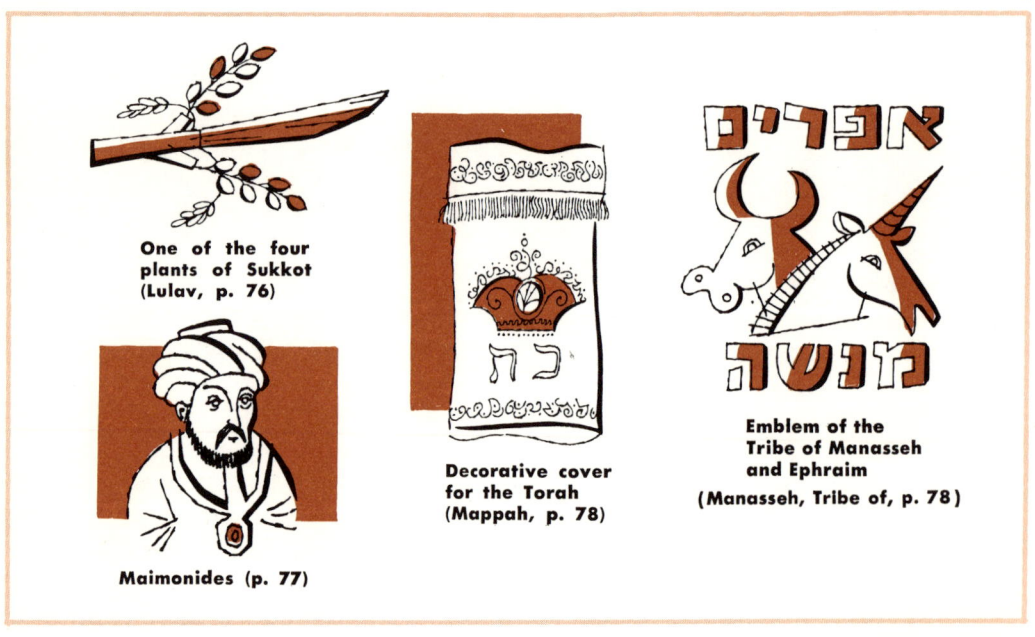

One of the four plants of Sukkot (Lulav, p. 76)

Maimonides (p. 77)

Decorative cover for the Torah (Mappah, p. 78)

Emblem of the Tribe of Manasseh and Ephraim (Manasseh, Tribe of, p. 78)

MAR
Hebrew word meaning "mister" or "sir."

MARIAMNE
The beautiful, gentle Hasmonean princess who was executed by her husband, Herod, the Idumean king of Judea, in 29 B.C.E.

MARRANOS
Jews, especially in Spain and Portugal during the Inquisition (the 14th and 15th centuries), forced to renounce their faith and practice Christianity or Islam. The Marranos secretly followed their own religion. The forced conversion of Jews has occurred in many lands ever since the seventh century.

MARRIAGE CONTRACT
see Ketubah

MAR SAMUEL
Samuel bar Abba, also called Yarhinaah (*astronomer*), one of the most important Babylonian scholars (about 180-257 C.E.); head of the academy of Nehardea. He and his colleague and friend, the great Rav, initiated work on the Babylonian Talmud (Gemara) which established Babylonia as the important center of Jewish life. Mar Samuel was also a physician and an astronomer. He drew up the first calendar for Babylonian Jewry. A humble man, he regarded Rav as superior to himself.

MAROR
Bitter herbs which are eaten at the Seder meal as a reminder of the bitterness of slavery.

MASHIAH
see Messiah

MASORAH
(*The handing down*) the work of preserving the traditional text of the Bible. Strict laws of Masorah have helped preserve the original text. The laws are still observed by the Soferim who write the Torah scrolls.

MASORETIC TEXT
The traditional text of the Bible, preserved by scholars who were called Masorites (or Masoretes). The Palestinian and Babylonian scholars, from about the 6th to the 10th centuries C.E., punctuated and fixed the present Masoretic text, but later scholars also made contributions.

MASSAH
A place near Mount Sinai, in the Sinai Desert, where Moses brought forth water from a rock for the thirsting, troubled Israelites.
(Exodus, chap. 17: 1-7)

MATRIARCHS
see Four Mothers

MATTANIAH
see Zedekiah

MATTATHIAS
Hasmonean priest of Modin, father of the five Maccabees. He inspired the victorious revolt against Antiochus Epiphanes of Syria (165 B.C.E.), and is one of the heroes of Hanukkah.

MATZAH
Flat, unleavened bread eaten during the Passover holiday. Matzah is eaten to commemorate the Exodus of the

Israelites from Egypt, when they fled so quickly that they did not have time for the dough of their bread to rise.

MEGIDDO
Ancient fortified town in the Plain of Jezreel where Barak defeated the Canaanites and where Josiah was killed by Pharaoh Necoh. King Solomon's stables were excavated at this site.

MEGILLAH
A small scroll of parchment mounted on one roller. The word generally refers to the Book of Esther, which is read on Purim.

MEGILLAT ESTHER
see Esther, Book of

MEGILLOT, THE FIVE
(*The scrolls*) five of the books of the last division *(Ketubim)* of the Bible. The Five Megillot are Song of Songs, Ruth, Lamentations, Ecclesiastes and Esther.

MEIR
Rabbi, great Tannaitic scholar and teacher of the 2nd century C.E., also called Baal Hanes (*miracle worker*), brilliant contributor to the Mishnah, disciple of Rabbi Akiba. Meir developed a distinctive manner of logical argument and a beautiful and concise style. Many popular sayings of Rabbi Meir are included in Ethics of the Fathers (*Pirke Avot*).

MELAVE MALKA
(*The seeing out of the Queen Sabbath*) the festivities accompanying a special meal after Havdalah, prolonging the joy of the Sabbath. Among many Jews, especially the Hasidim, this is a time for joyous singing and prayer, as they usher out the Sabbath, and begin a new workday week with hope and good wishes.

MENAHEM
One of the last kings of the Kingdom of Israel (about 741-737 B.C.E.). He

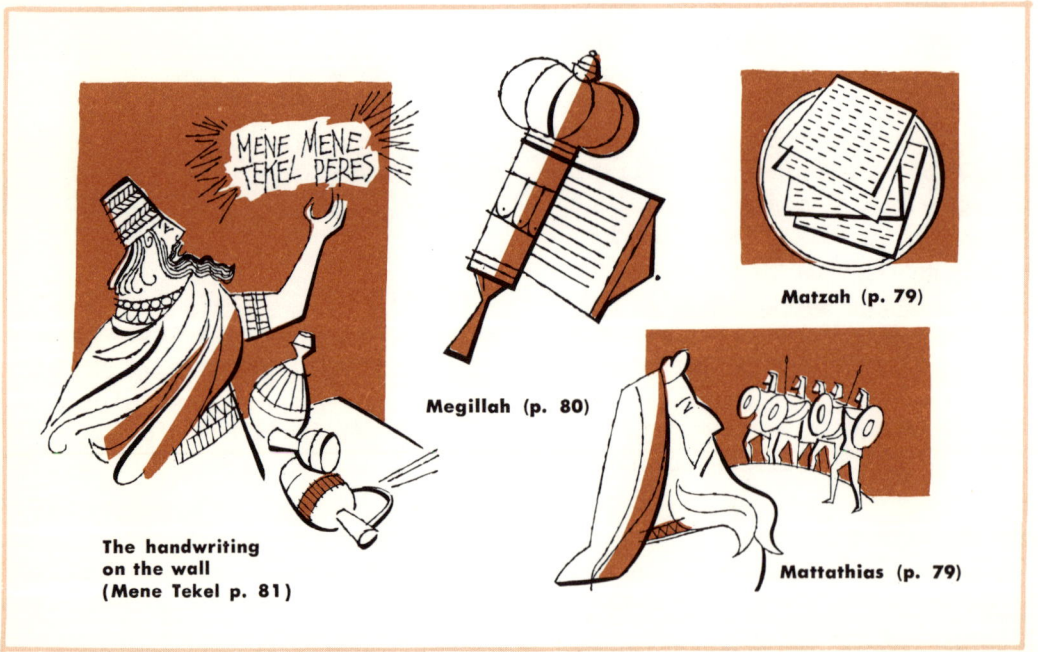

The handwriting on the wall (Mene Tekel p. 81)

Megillah (p. 80)

Matzah (p. 79)

Mattathias (p. 79)

assassinated and succeeded Shallum. Menahem cruelly taxed the people to collect a large tribute for Assyria and contributed to Israel's eventual annexation by Assyria. The prophet Hosea described the times of Menahem.

(Kings II, chap. 15: 14-22)

MENE TEKEL

(Mene, Mene, Tekel Upharsin) handwriting that appeared on the wall at King Belshazzar's feast. Daniel interpreted these words to mean that God had judged the king and found him wanting, and that the overthrow of the Babylonian Kingdom by the Medes and Persians was approaching. Belshazzar was slain that night, and soon the Persians took Babylonia.

(Daniel, chap. 5: 25-28)

MENORAH

Originally a seven-branched candlestick that was kept in the Tabernacle and later in the Temple in Jerusalem. It has become one of the important symbols of Judaism. It has never been reproduced in its seven-branched form; instead, six- or eight-branched Menorot are used in the synagogues.

MENORAH, HANUKKAH

An eight-branched candlelabrum with an extra branch (called the Shamos, which is used to kindle the other lights.) The Menorah is lit (one light the first night, two the second, etc.) in commemoration of the jug of oil that burned for eight days and nights after the cleansing of the Temple. The Menorah is considered a symbol of freedom and of the light of God that survives all difficulties.

MESHACH

see Shadrach

MESOPOTAMIA

Fertile land between the Euphrates and the Tigris where the great Babylonian, Assyrian and Syrian empires flourished. Today this land is part of Iraq.

MESSIAH

(*Mashiah, anointed one*) a man who, it is prophesied, will appear at the dawn of the Golden Age, when peace will reign throughout the world and when the holiness of God and the brotherhood of man will be recognized by all. It is envisioned that the Messiah will be a man of great wisdom and dedication, a prophet of God, and will be of the tribe of Judah, a descendant of David.

METHUSELAH

Son of Enoch; grandfather of Noah. It is said he reached the great age of 969 years.

(Genesis, chap. 5: 25-27)

MEZUZAH

A wooden or metal case in which the Shema and another passage from Deuteronomy are hand written on a tiny scroll. The Mezuzah is placed on the right side of doorposts of homes and synagogues, in accordance with a Biblical commandment.

(Deut., chap. 6: 9)

MICAH

Sixth of the Books of Twelve (Minor) Prophets of the Bible. Micah, a humble peasant from Gath, prophesied in Judah at the time of Isaiah. He cried out against injustice and dishonesty. "What doth the Lord require of thee," said Micah, "save to do justice, and to love mercy, and to walk humbly with thy God?" Micah, as Isaiah, envisioned a future time when war would cease and all men would be at peace.

MICHAEL
Angel and messenger of God, patron angel of Israel.

MICHAL
Daughter of King Saul, one of the wives of David. Michal helped David escape when Saul pursued him.
(Samuel I, chap. 19: 11-17)

MIDIAN
1. Land of the Midianites (and Kenites) in the Sinai Desert. Moses, after slaying the Egyptian taskmaster, fled to Midian where he found refuge with Jethro.

2. Son of Abraham and Keturah, ancestor of the Midianites.

MIDIANITES
Descendants of Midian, also called Ishmaelites, Bedouin tribe of the Sinai Desert, south of Edom, related to the Kenites. Midianites were among the first to domesticate camels. At the time of the Judges, the Midianites were decisively beaten by Gideon.

MIDRASH
Form of commentary on a Biblical passage, much like a sermon. There are two kinds of Midrashim; the Midrash Halachah, which tries to clarify a point of law, and the Midrash Aggadah, which illustrates a spiritual or ethical point. Both kinds of Midrashim seek to interpret the deeper meaning of a Biblical passage. Midrashic writings on all parts of the Bible have been collected over a thousand-year span.

MILCHIG
Milk and foods such as cheese, rennet and butter derived from milk, which, traditionally, cannot be eaten together with fleishig (*meat*).

see Dietary Laws

MINHAH
The Afternoon Service, the third (in the Jewish calendar, the day begins after sunset) of the three daily services. The Minhah prayers are recited in the afternoon up to sunset.

MINNIG
see Parve

MINOR PROPHETS
see Prophets, Twelve

MINYAN
Number or quorum. A minimum of ten men, above the age of thirteen, are required for public worship.

MIRIAM
Sister of Moses and Aaron, prophetess. She watched over the baby Moses in the bulrushes of the Nile and arranged for Pharaoh's daughter, who found the baby, to employ Jochebed, Moses' mother, as his nurse. Miriam led the Hebrew women in grateful singing and dancing after the crossing of the Red Sea.
(Exodus, chap. 2: 1-9; chap. 15: 20-21)

MISHLE
see Proverbs, Book of

MISHNAH
Basic part of the Talmud, first Jewish code of law since the Torah, the core of "Oral Torah," based on the Torah. It consists of laws and com-

mentaries passed on for generations by word of mouth. They were collected and edited by Judah Hanasi (about 200 C.E.). The teachers and scholars whose decisions and discussions are recorded in the Mishnah are called Tannaim.

MISHNAH, DIVISIONS OF
see Sedarim

MISHNEH TORAH
1. (*Repetition of the Law*) early Hebrew name for Deuteronomy.

2. Name of Maimonides' great code of Talmudic laws, systematically arranged and codified, also known as Yad Hazakah (*Strong Hand*).

see Maimonides

MITZVAH
(*A commandment*). There are 613 commandments listed in the Bible; 248 positive commandments, and 365 negative. The fulfillment of these commandments is not for material gain but to perfect moral character and to express love of God. Mitzvah colloquially means "a good deed."

MIZRAH
1. (*East*) the east wall of the synagogue. The congregation usually faces east, as a symbol of its hopes for the restoration of the Temple on Mount Zion in Jerusalem.

2. A drawing on parchment or paper, or a tapestry, hung on the east wall of a room.

MITZRAIM
1. Hebrew name for Egypt.

2. Noah's grandson, ancestor of the Hamitic peoples.

see Egypt

MOAB
Ancient kingdom of the Moabites, east of the Jordan and the Dead Sea, opposite Jericho. There were alternate periods of peace and warfare between Israel and Moab. Ruth, David's ancestor, was a Moabite. Moab was destroyed by Assyria.

MODIN
Village in the Judean hills, home of the Hasmonean priest Mattathias and his sons, the Maccabees. The Maccabean revolt started in Modin.

MOED
see Sedarim

MOHEL
One who performs the ceremony of circumcision. The person performing this function must be qualified both by piety and training.

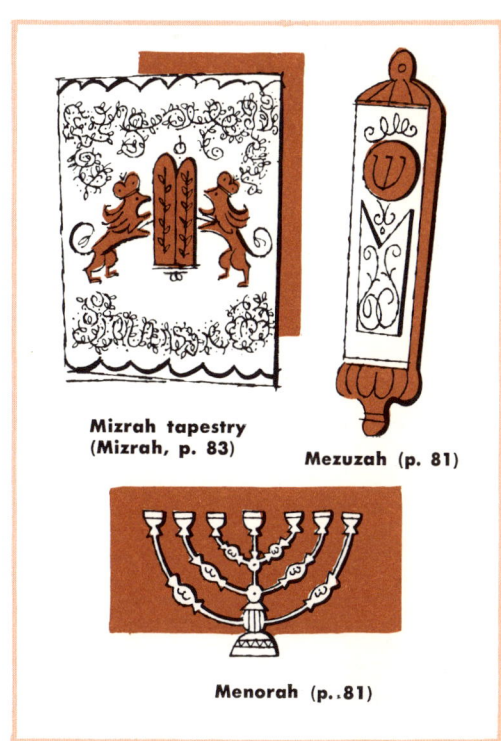

Mizrah tapestry (Mizrah, p. 83)

Mezuzah (p. 81)

Menorah (p..81)

MONTH

(*Hodesh*) in the Jewish calendar a month consists of 29 or 30 days, the period of time between one new moon and the next.

see Rosh Hodesh

MONTHS, JEWISH

The Jewish year begins with Rosh Hashanah on the first of Tishri. There are 12 months in the Jewish civil calendar: Tishri, Heshvan, Kislev, Tevet, Shevat, Adar, Nisan, Iyar, Sivan, Tammuz, Av and Elul. In leap years a 13th month is added: Adar Sheni or Veadar.

see Calendar, Jewish

MONUMENT

see Tombstones

MORDECAI

Guardian and cousin of Queen Esther. He once saved King Ahasuerus from assassination. He influenced Esther to save the Jews of Persia from Haman's plot against the Jews. After Haman was hanged, Mordecai became second in command to the king.

MORIAH, MOUNT

The mountain where God tested Abraham by commanding him to sacrifice his son Isaac. In David's time, Mount Moriah was called Mount Zion. Later Mount Zion was also called Temple Mount (*Har Habayit*), because the Temple of Jerusalem stood there.

MORNING SERVICE

see Shaharit

MOSES

Son of Amram and Jochebed, brother of Miriam and Aaron, husband of Zipporah, father of Gershom and Eliezer. Moses was the greatest leader and prophet of Israel. He led the Israelites out of Egyptian bondage and received the Ten Commandments at Mount Sinai. He explained God's commandments to the people and installed Israel's first priests. Moses did not live to enter the Promised Land. His burial place on Mount Nebo, in the land of Moab, is not known. Moses was of the tribe of Levi.

MOSES BEN MAIMON

see Maimonides

MOUNT GERIZIM

see Gerizim, Mount

MOUNT GILBOA

see Gilboa, Mount

MOUNT HOR

see Hor, Mount

MOUNT NEBO

see Nebo, Mount

MOUNT SINAI

see Sinai, Mount

MOUNT TABOR

see Tabor, Mount

MUSAF

(*Additional Service*) a collection of prayers recited after the Morning Prayer (*Shaharit*) and the reading of the Torah. Musaf is said on Rosh Hodesh, Sabbath and on holidays.

MYRTLE
see Hadas

NABOTH
The owner of a vineyard which King Ahab desired. Queen Jezebel aided Ahab to secure the vineyard by falsely accusing Naboth of blasphemy and having him stoned to death. The prophet Elijah rebuked Ahab for this cruel injustice.

(Kings I, chap. 21)

NADAB
1. Oldest son of Aaron; one of Israel's first priests.

(Leviticus, chap. 10:1-7)

2. Second king of the northern Kingdom of Israel (about 915-914 B.C.E.), son of Jeroboam. He warred against the Philistines. Nadab was assassinated by Baasa, who succeeded him.

(Kings I, chap. 15:25-31)

NAHUM
Seventh of the Books of the Twelve (Minor) Prophets of the Bible. Nahum prophesied the fall of the mighty Assyrians and the destruction of Nineveh, the great Assyrian capital.

NAOMI
Israelite mother-in-law of Ruth the Moabite; ancestor of King David. The Book of Ruth tells how Naomi, after the death of her husband and sons, returned to Bethlehem, followed by the faithful Ruth.

NAPHTALI
Sixth son of Jacob, second son of Bilhah, ancestor of the tribe of Naphtali.

NAPHTALI, TRIBE OF
One of the tribes of Israel. Its territory was in northern Galilee. Naphtali's emblem was a deer; its banner was wine-color. The stone representing Naphtali in the high priest's breastplate was probably an amethyst.

NASHIM
see Sedarim

NASI
(Prince, eminence—referred to by the Romans as "patriarch") originally the head of the Great Sanhedrin.

Moses (p. 84)

Emblem of the Tribe of Naphtali (Naphtali, Tribe of, p. 85)

Mordecai (p. 84)

From the time of the destruction of the Temple until the 5th century, the Nasi, who was always a great Palestinian scholar, was the recognized spiritual leader of all Jews, the spokesman of the Jewish community of the land of Israel and head of its highest court. This system of leadership is often referred to as the Patriarchate. The title Nasi was inherited by the scholarly descendants of Hillel.

see Zugot

NATHAN
Prophet, advisor to King David and King Solomon. Nathan helped plan the building of the Temple. He anointed King Solomon.
(Samuel II, chap. 7: 1-17; chap. 12: 1-25; Kings I, chap. 1)

NEBO, MOUNT
A mountain in Moab. From its heights, the aging leader and prophet of Israel, Moses, saw the Promised Land of Israel before he died.
(Deut., chap. 32: 48-52; chap. 34)

NEBUCHADNEZZAR II
Also spelled Nebuchadrezzar, King of Babylonia (about 604-561 B.C.E.), destroyed the First Temple and Jerusalem. He conquered Judah and led its people into captivity to Babylonia.
(Kings II, chaps. 24-25)

NEHARDEA
Oldest of the three most famous Babylonian academies, founded in the 2nd century C.E. It contributed greatly to the Babylonian Talmud.

NEHEMIAH
Governor of Judea, helped restore the religious faith of the community of Judea. Nehemiah, favorite and cupbearer of King Artaxerxes of Persia, of wealthy and noble background, set an example for all the citizens of Jerusalem when he freed the poor of their debts. He helped rebuild the walls of the city. Together with Ezra, he inspired the people to make a new covenant with God.

NEHEMIAH, BOOK OF
With the Book of Ezra, the second book of historical writings of the 3rd division *(Ketubim)* of the Bible. The book is a record of the life and times of Nehemiah.

NEILAH
(Closing) the concluding service on Yom Kippur. It is the climax of a day of prayer, and is conducted in a mood of solemnity and reverence.

NER TAMID
(*Eternal light*) the light that burns continuously before the ark in the synagogue, a symbolic continuation of the holy light that burned in the Temple. The Ner Tamid reminds the congregation of the continuous presence of God.

NES GADOL HAYAH SHAM
(*A great miracle happened there*) refers to the rededication of the ancient Temple in Jerusalem, when it was liberated by Judah Maccabee and his followers. The first letter of each word of this saying appears on the four sides of the dreydel.

NEVI'IM
see Prophets

NEW MOON
see Rosh Hodesh

NEZIKIM

see Sedarim

NIGGUN

(Melody, music) refers to the musical form for the chanting of prayers and the wordless songs sung by the Hasidim and others.

NINEVEH

Ancient capital of the great Assyrian empire. Both Israel and Judah paid tribute to Nineveh. The prophet Jonah was commanded to travel to this city to preach. Nineveh was destroyed by the Babylonians and was never rebuilt.

(Jonah, chap. 3)

NISAN

Seventh month in the Jewish calendar.

see Months, Jewish

NOAH

Grandson of Methuselah; a righteous man whom God saved from the Flood. Noah built the ark in which he and his family and a pair of each species of animals were saved. After the Flood a rainbow appeared which was a token of God's covenant with Noah and all living creatures to never again destroy a whole generation.

(Genesis, chaps. 6-9)

NOD

The land east of Eden where Cain fled after he murdered his brother Abel. Cain lived in Nod as a wanderer and vagabond.

(Genesis, chap. 4: 16)

NUMBERS, BOOK OF

(Bamidbar) fourth of the Biblical Five Books of Moses (the Torah). Numbers records the 40 years of Israel's wanderings in the wilderness. Its 36 chapters are divided into 10 portions for weekly Sabbath readings. Its name is derived from an event it describes, the "numbering," or counting of the Israelites.

OBADIAH

1. Fourth Book of the Twelve (Minor) Prophets of the Bible. Obadiah prophesied the destruction of Edom and the restoration of Israel.

2. Ahab's steward who courageously risked his life hiding many prophets

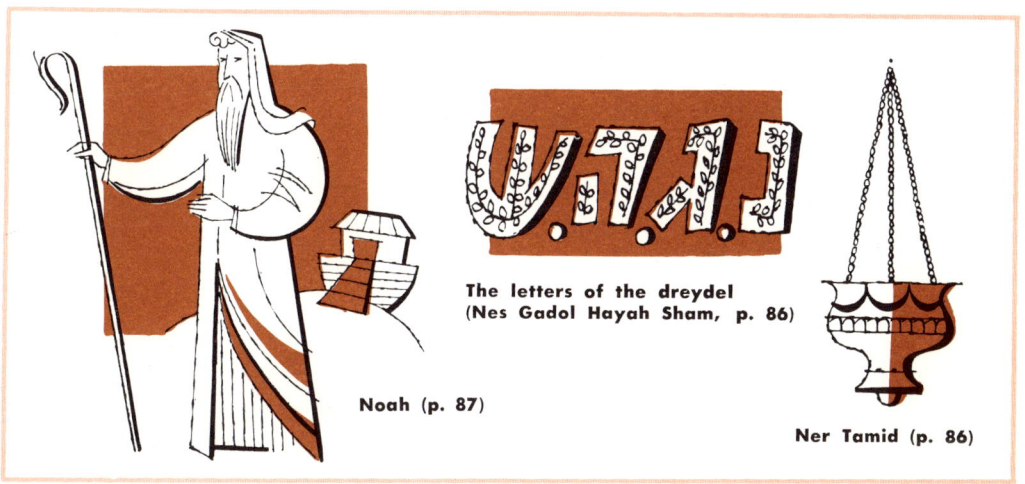

Noah (p. 87)

The letters of the dreydel (Nes Gadol Hayah Sham, p. 86)

Ner Tamid (p. 86)

in caves to save them from Queen Jezebel's persecutions.

(Kings I, chap. 18: 1-16)

OHEL MOED

Hebrew name for the Tabernacle that housed the Ark during Israel's wanderings in the desert.

see Tabernacle

OHOLIAB

Assistant to Bezalel in the building of the Ark and the Tabernacle.

(Exodus, chap. 31:6; chap. 35:34)

see Bezalel

OMER

Measure of grain in ancient Israel. An Omer of grain from the first harvest was taken to the Temple as a thanksgiving offering. The first harvest of the year took place during the 49 days between Passover and Shavuot, and was called the period of Omer or Sefirah (*counting*). No one ate of the new grain until the giving of Omer.

(Lev., chap. 23: 9-17)

OMRI

Sixth king of the northern Kingdom of Israel (about 889-875 B.C.E.), father of Ahab. Israel flourished under Omri's reign. He established trade with the Phoenicians and reconquered Moab. Omri left the old capital Tirzah and built Samaria, the new capital city.

(Kings I, chap. 16: 15-28)

ONEG SHABBAT

(*Joy of Sabbath, rejoicing of the Sabbath*) an hour of social gatherings and cultural activities on Friday evenings or Sabbath afternoons. The modern form of Oneg Shabbat was initiated in Israel (then Palestine) by the poet C. N. Bialik. Refreshments are often served for Oneg Shabbat, probably deriving from the ancient custom of the Se'udah Shelishit, the third and last prescribed Sabbath meal, which was often accompanied by festivities and singing.

ONKELOS

see Targum

OPHRAH

Ancient town near Shechem where Gideon the Judge lived and was buried.

(Judges, chap. 6: 11)

ORAL TORAH

Post-Biblical laws founded on the laws of the (written) Torah. The laws of the Oral Torah were passed on by word of mouth, from generation to generation, until they were collected and edited in the Mishnah. The Oral Torah—the Mishnah—is the basis of the Talmud.

ORDINATION

(*Semikhah*) the authority given to rabbis to decide on questions of Jewish law. In modern times, rabbis receive ordination after completing an intensive course of study at a seminary or a Yeshiva.

ORTHODOX JUDAISM

see Judaism

OTHNIEL

Son of Kenaz; Caleb's younger brother, of the tribe of Judah, first Judge of Israel. He delivered Israel from King Cushan-rishathaim of Aram.

(Judges, chap. 3: 7-11)

PADDAN-ARAM

Region along the upper Euphrates where the city of Haran was situated. Haran was the home of Rebekah and Laban and his daughters, Leah and Rachel.

PALESTINE

Name for the land of Israel, the territory west of the Jordan from Dan to Beer-sheba. The name is a derivation from the word Philistine and was first used by the Greeks, and later by the Romans (Palestina). The name is not mentioned in the Bible.

PALESTINIAN ACADEMIES

see Academies, Palestinian

PALESTINIAN TALMUD

see Talmud, Palestinian

PALM

see Lulav

PARADISE

see Garden of Eden

PARAN

Wilderness in the Sinai Peninsula near the Gulf of Aqaba where Hagar and Ishmael lived after they were cast out of the household of Abraham.

(Genesis, chap. 21: 21)

PARASHAH

(*Sidrah*) the portion of the Torah read on the Sabbath. The Sefer Torah does not have chapters. It is divided into 54 portions (*parshiyot*) which are read during the year.

PAROKHET

The curtain which hangs before the ark in the synagogue. It is usually made of beautiful cloth and is artistically decorated. It often bears the letters Kaf and Tav, the initials of Keter Torah *(Crown of the Torah)*. Its color is usually red or blue. On the High Holy Days a white Parokhet is used.

PARVE

Also called minnig, foods such as eggs, fish, fruit and vegetables which, according to Jewish dietary laws, can be eaten with either milk or meat dishes. These foods are considered neutral *(parve)*.

PASSOVER

(*Pesach*) one of the three harvest and pilgrimage festivals, the holiday that marks the beginning of Spring. Passover celebrates the deliverance of the Israelites from Egyptian slavery. The name of the holiday is derived from the event of the angel of death "passing over" the Israelite houses when every Egyptian first-born son was smitten. Passover is also called the Feast of Freedom and the Feast of Matzot.

(Exodus, chap. 12)

PATRIARCHATE

Refers to the leadership of the Nasim (the scholarly heads of the great Palestinian academies) who led the Jewish community of the land of Israel after the destruction of the Second Temple and until about 425 C.E. Their spiritual and legal authority was generally accepted and supported by voluntary taxation by Jews throughout the ancient world.

PATRIARCHS, THE THREE

The fathers of the Jewish people, Abraham, Isaac and Jacob.

THE WORLD OF ABRAHAM, ISAAC, JACOB AND JOSEPH
JACOB RETURNS FROM HARAN
SEA OF KINNERETH
JOSEPH SOLD BY HIS BROTHERS
THE GREAT SEA
JACOB BECOMES "ISRAEL"
RIVER
SHECHEM
PENIEL
JABBOK RIVER
WHERE JACOB DREAMED
JORDAN
AMMON
PERMANENT HOME OF ABRAHAM
BETH-EL
THE SCENE OF THE SACRIFICE OF ISAAC
MAMRE
MT. MORIAH
DEAD SEA
THE CHIEF PHILISTINE CAMP
HEBRON
ARNON RIVER
MOAB
WHERE THE PATRIARCHS WERE BURIED
GOMORRAH
WHERE ISAAC DWELT MANY YEARS
SODOM
PROBABLE LOCATIONS OF BURIED CITIES
BEER-SHEBA
EDOM
N
W
E
S
THE NEGEV

PEKAH

One of the last kings of the northern Kingdom of Israel (about 736-734 B.C.E.), overthrew Pekahiah. He organized an alliance against the mighty Assyrians; he also warred against Judah. Pekah was overthrown by Hoshea.

(Kings II, chap. 15: 23-31)

PEKAHIAH

One of the last kings of Israel (about 737-736 B.C.E.), son of Menahem. He was assassinated and succeeded by Pekah.

(Kings II, chap. 15: 23-26)

PENITENCE, PRAYERS OF

see Selihot

PENTATEUCH

Greek name for Humash; the Five Books of Moses; the Torah.

PERSIA

Great empire of antiquity that overthrew Babylonia, ruled over Media, Lydia, Persia and Babylonia and their possessions. The Persian kings, Cyrus the Great and Darius I, helped the Jews return to Judea and rebuild the Temple. Persia's King Xerxes was probably King Ahasuerus, husband of Esther. Persia was overthrown by Alexander the Great of Macedonia. Today the original territory of Persia is modern Iran.

PESACH

see Passover

PEZUKE DEZIMRA

(*Passages of Song*) passages from the Books of Chronicles and Psalms recited before the morning service (*Shaharit*).

PHARAOH

(*The Great House*) originally name and title of honor of the rulers of Egypt. Pharaoh later came to mean simply "King." The Pharaoh at the time of the Exodus was Ramses II.

** THE THREE PATRIARCHS AND THE FOUR MOTHERS OF ISRAEL.

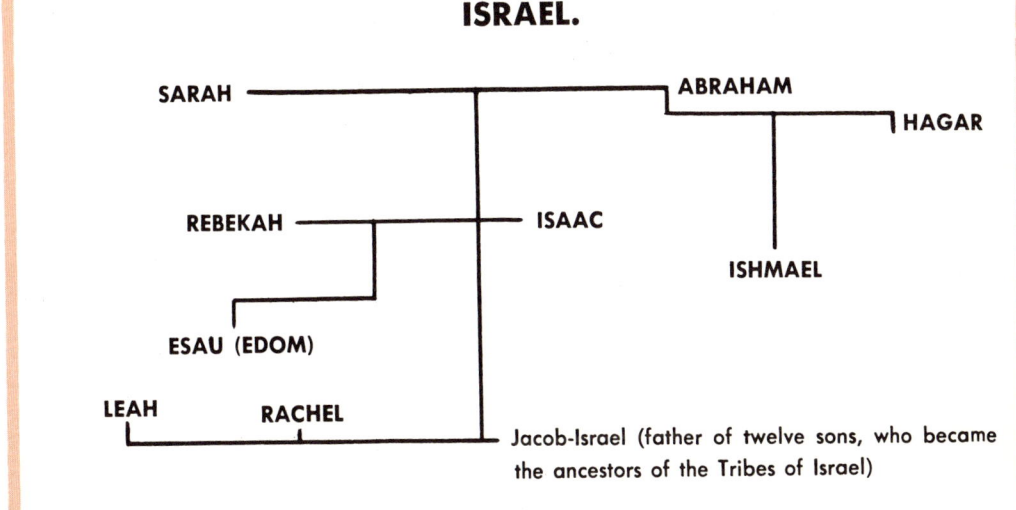

PHARISEES

(*Perushim*, probably meaning "separate ones") Jewish party (or sect) during the reign of the Hasmoneans and at the time of the Roman rule of Judea (end of the 2nd century B.C.E. through the 1st century C.E.). They believed in strict adherence to the laws of the Torah and based their interpretations on Oral Torah, teachings of Ezra and the Soferim. They were bitter opponents of the Sadducees. The Pharisees helped lay the foundation for the Talmudic tradition.

PHILISTIA

see Philistines

PHILISTINES

Neighbors and bitter enemies of Israel. Their land, Philistia, consisting of five powerful federated city-states, Gaza, Ashkelon, Ashdod, Ekron and Gath, extended along the fertile southern coast of Palestine. The Philistines conquered Israel in the late period of the Judges (Samson, Eli) and captured the Ark. Saul and David fought the Philistines, David finally conquering them.

PHINEHAS

1. Third high priest of Israel, son of Eleazar, grandson of Aaron, zealous opponent of idol worship. After the Israelites conquered Canaan, Phinehas lived in Ephraim.

(Numbers, chap. 25: 6-13; Joshua, chap. 24: 33)

2. One of the sons of the Judge and high priest Eli, regarded unworthy to succeed his father. Phinehas and his brother Hophni fell in the battle against the Philistines when the Ark was captured.

(Samuel I, chap. 2: 12-35; chap. 4: 11-22)

PHOENICIANS

Neighbors of Israel who lived in the north, along the northeast Mediterranean coast, flanked by the Lebanon Mountains. Their wealthy capital was Tyre. David and Solomon befriended

Phoenician (p. 92)   Pharaoh (p. 91)   Omer (p. 88)   Parokhet (p. 89)   Philistine (Philistines, p. 92)

these great travelers, seafarers and merchants. They assisted Solomon in building up his fleet and his trade and they supplied the beautiful cedars of Lebanon for the construction of the Temple. Later, Phoenician settlers founded Carthage, great adversary of Rome.

PHYLACTERIES
see Tefillin

PIDYON HABEN
(The redemption of the first-born son) a ceremony that takes place 30 days after the birth of the first son. As a first son belongs traditionally to the service of God, he is symbolically redeemed by his father by an offering of money (5 shekels) to a Cohen, or a Levite, as the Levites and Cohanim were dedicated (instead of the first-born) to the service of God.

(Numbers, chap. 18: 15-16)

PILGRIMAGE FESTIVALS, THREE
see Shalosh Regalim

PIRKE AVOT
(Ethics of the Fathers) one of the best known parts of the Mishnah, wise sayings of the great rabbis and teachers; often read or studied on Sabbath afternoons, starting with the Sabbath after Passover until the Sabbath before Rosh Hashanah. Selections from Pirke Avot are included in many Siddurim.

PISGAH
Mountain in ancient Moab, northwest of Mount Nebo, often referred to as part of Mount Nebo and as the place where Moses died and was buried.

(Deuteronomy, chap. 34:1)

PITHOM AND RAAMSES
The two Egyptian cities built by the enslaved Israelites, probably for the Pharaoh Ramses II. Pithom and Raamses were "store-cities," where great store-houses were built and filled with food and Pharaoh's treasures. At Pithom, modern archeologists have uncovered massive walls built of "bricks without straw," as described in the Biblical Book of Exodus.

(Exodus, chap. 1:11)

PIYUT
A religious poem. Many beautiful piyutim are part of the synagogue service.

PLAGUES, THE TEN
The ten successive plagues visited upon Egypt to compel Pharaoh to set the Israelites free. A recital of these plagues is a traditional part of the Passover Seder.

(Exodus, chap. 7:14-chap. 12:36)

POTIPHAR
Official at Pharaoh's court who bought the young Joseph from the Midianites. He made Joseph overseer of his household. His wife falsely accused Joseph and caused him to be thrown into prison.

(Genesis, chap. 39)

POTI-PHERA
Egyptian dignitary and priest of On; father of Asenath, Joseph's wife.

(Genesis, chap. 41:45)

PRAYER BOOK
see Mahzor

see Siddur

PRAYER SHAWL
see Tallit

PREACHER
see Maggid

PRIESTLY BLESSING
see Birkat Cohanim

PRIESTS
see Cohanim

PROMISED LAND
see Holy Land

PROPHETS
Men of God *(Nevi'im)* who conveyed God's will to the people. They fought idol worship and inspired the people to preserve their faith. They often rebuked men of power, kings and priests who were idolatrous and cruel. Some of the prophets traveled in groups through the land and preached to the people. They tried to make the people understand the deeper meanings of their religion. They taught that to bring sacrifices was not as important as to love God and to be just to men. Their histories and their writings are recorded in the Books of Prophets of the Bible.

PROPHETS, BOOKS OF
(Nevi'im) second major division of the Bible, consisting of:

1. The Books of Early Prophets *(Nevi'im Rishonim)*, which include Joshua, Judges, Samuel, I and II, and Kings, I and II. These books tell the history of the Jewish people from the time of Joshua until the destruction of the First Temple, 586 B.C.E.

2. The Books of Later Prophets *(Nevi'im Aharonim)*, which contain, often in beautiful literary form, the prophecies and orations of the Later Prophets. Later Prophets consist of four books, one of each of the three Major Prophets, and the Book of the Twelve (Minor) Prophets.

PROPHETS, MAJOR
The three great prophets, Isaiah, Jeremiah and Ezekiel, whose writings were recorded in Later Prophets *(Nevi'im Aharonim)*, in the Books of Isaiah, Jeremiah and Ezekiel.

PROPHETS, MINOR
see Prophets, Twelve

PROPHETS, TWELVE
Also called Minor Prophets. Their works are shorter than those of the Major Prophets, and together constitute the Fourth Book of Later Prophets. These Twelve Prophets are: Hosea, Joel, Amos, Obadiah, Jonah, Micah, Nahum, Habakkuk, Zephaniah, Haggai, Zechariah and Malachi.

PROVERBS, BOOK OF
(Mishle) second book of the 3rd division *(Ketubim)* of the Bible. It consists of a collection of wise sayings ascribed to King Solomon.

PSALMS, BOOK OF
(Tehillim) first and longest of the three poetical books of the 3rd division *(Ketubim)* of the Bible, a collection of 150 beautiful poems. The book is also called the Psalms of David, though some of the poems were probably written by other people.

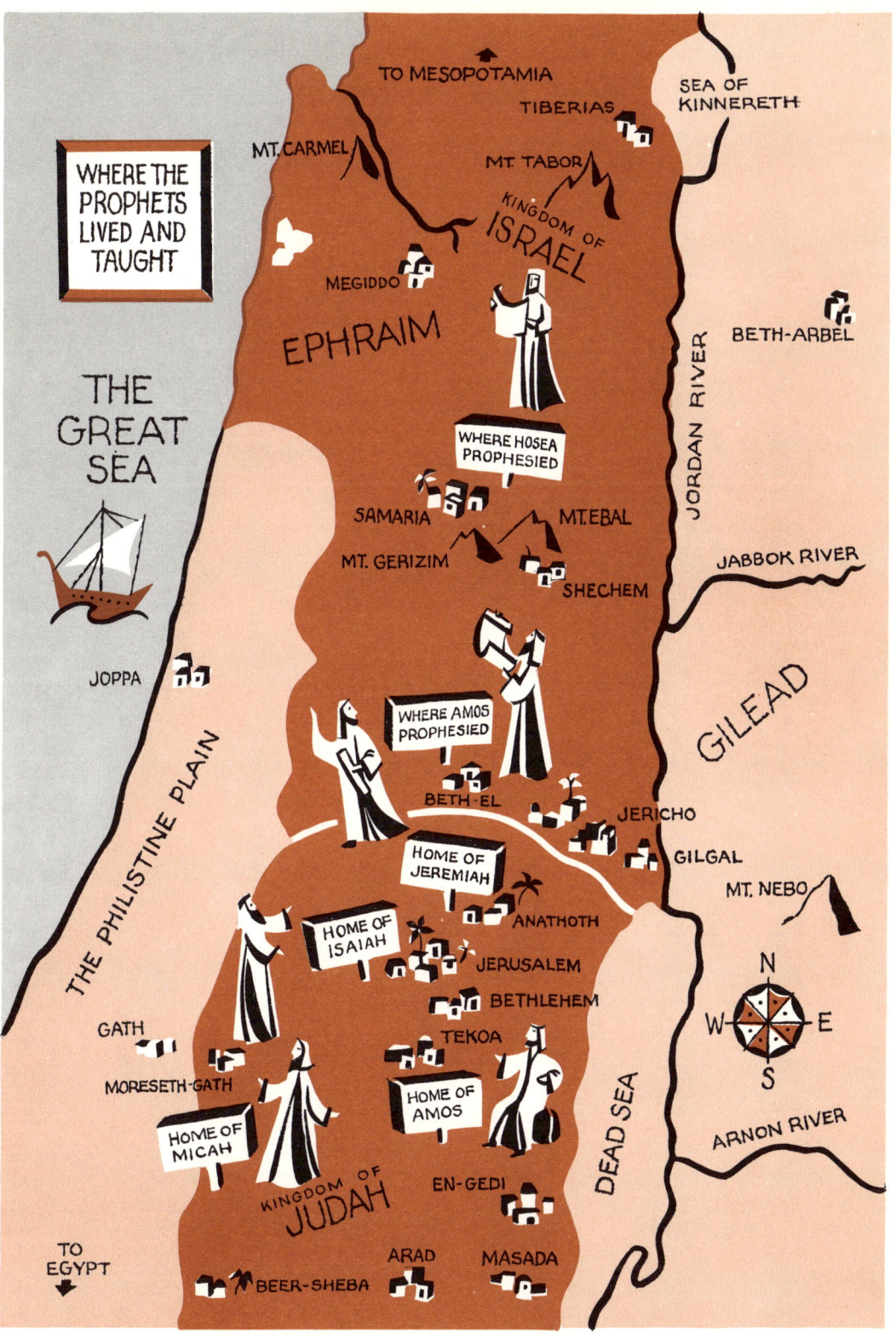

PSEUDO-EPIGRAPHA
Books similar to Biblical writings, but excluded from the Bible. Many of these books were written under the names of famous Biblical figures, to make them more acceptable.

PULPIT
see Bimah

PUMPADITA
(Also Pumbeditha) one of the three most famous Babylonian Talmudic academies, founded in the 3rd century C.E. and for eight centuries a foremost seat of Jewish learning.

PURIM
(*Feast of Lots*) a holiday that celebrates the escape of the Jews of Persia from Haman's evil plot to destroy them. Haman, a favorite of King Ahasuerus, was angered by Mordecai, a cousin of Queen Esther, who refused to bow down before him. Haman cast lots to choose the day of destruction of Mordecai and all the Jews of Persia, and tricked Ahasuerus to give his approval. The Book of Esther, which is read on Purim, recounts the courage of Queen Esther, who risked her life to expose Haman to the King. Purim is a joyous holiday and is celebrated with parties, costume plays and Shalach Manot.

RAAMSES
see Pithom and Raamses

RABBAN
Honorary title of the presidents of the Sanhedrin in their capacity as teachers of law.

RABBANA
Honorary title bestowed upon Exilarchs and outstanding Talmudic scholars in Babylonia.

RABBENU TAM
see Tosafot

RABBI
1. The spiritual leader of a congregation ordained by a theological seminary or a Yeshiva. The rabbi is expected to be devoted to the principles of Judaism, to be a scholar, and to lead an exemplary life. In the past a rabbi was ordained by another rabbi of great repute. The meaning of the Hebrew word "Rabbi" is "my master" or "my teacher."

2. Honorary name of Judah Hanasi.

see Judah Hanasi

RABINA BAR HUNA
Great scholar (Amora) who, with Ashi, collected and edited the Babylonian Talmud. Rabina was Ashi's assistant and, after Ashi's death, his successor. Rabina died in 499 C.E.

RABBINISM
The tradition of safekeeping, study and interpretation of the Torah, founded by Ezra and the Soferim and carried on to the present day by rabbis, scholars and teachers. The greatest work embodying this tradition is the Talmud.

RACHEL
Younger daughter of Laban, favorite wife of Jacob, sister of Leah. She was the mother of Joseph and Benjamin. Her tomb is near Ramah and Bethlehem. She was one of the Four Mothers of Israel.

(Genesis, chaps. 29-30; 35: 16-20)

RAMAH
1. City in the territory of Ephraim, home of Samuel.

2. A fortress between Judah and Israel, near Jerusalem. Rachel's grave is near Ramah.

RAMBAM
see Maimonides

RAMOTH-GILEAD
City of Refuge, in the territory of Gad, in Gilead, east of the Jordan; scene of many battles between Israel and Aram.

see Cities of Refuge

RAMSES II
Pharaoh at the time of the Exodus of the Jews from Egypt.

RAPHAEL
Angel and messenger of God, healer and performer of miracles.

RASHI
(Rabbi Solomon ben Isaac) famous for his commentaries on Torah and Talmud, born in Troyes, France, 1040, died in Troyes in 1105. He studied at the great Yeshiva of Worms. At the age of 25 he became the unsalaried rabbi of Troyes (he earned his livelihood as a vintner and farmer). Rashi founded a Yeshiva in Troyes. Until the end of his life, he worked on his brilliant commentaries, which today are still indispensable to students and scholars of the Torah and Talmud. Rashi was a humble and unassuming man of great purity.

RAV
1. (*Master, teacher*) title of Babylonian scholars and rabbis who were not ordained in the land of Israel. The Orthodox rabbi of today is sometimes referred to as Rav.

2. Honorary name of Abba Arekha, great Babylonian scholar.

see Abba Arekha

RAVINA
see Rabina

The Book of Esther (Purim, p. 96)

Ramses II (p. 97)

Rashi (p. 97)

97

REBEKAH

Daughter of Bethuel; wife of Isaac, mother of Jacob and Esau, one of the Four Mothers of Israel. Believing Jacob more deserving than Esau, she helped him to deceive ancient, blind Isaac and to receive the first-born's blessing instead of Esau. Rebekah was buried in the Cave of Machpelah.

(Genesis, chaps. 24 and 27)

RECONSTRUCTIONISM

see Judaism

RED SEA

The oceanic gulf which extends from the Indian Ocean to the Gulf of Suez, the scene of the miraculous crossing by the Israelites, under Moses' guidance, in their escape from Egypt and Pharaoh's army. In Hebrew the Red Sea is called "Yam Suf" (*Sea of Reeds*).

(Exodus, chaps. 14-15)

REFORM JUDAISM

see Judaism

REHOBOAM

Son of Solomon, became king at the age of 16 (about 937-920 B.C.E.). He arrogantly ignored the people's plea for easing their taxes and burdens. The northern tribes revolted and, under Jeroboam, founded the northern Kingdom of Israel. The southern tribes, consisting of the tribes of Judah and Benjamin, remained loyal to Rehoboam and formed the Kingdom of Judah.

(Kings I, chap. 12; chap. 14: 21-31)

RESPONSA

(*Teshuvot*) answers given by Talmudic scholars (originally of the great academies) to questions (*Shealot*) concerning legal and religious problems of communities or individuals. The first Responsa were collected at the time of the Ga'onim. Responsa were recorded throughout the centuries and are still written today. Jewish thought and history of various periods and of many lands are mirrored in the collections of Responsa.

RESTORATION

The name used to refer to the period after the return of the Jews from Babylonian Exile to Judea (about 538-432 B.C.E.). During the time of the Restoration, Jerusalem was rebuilt and the foundation was laid for the Second Temple and for the Second Commonwealth. At this time Ezra and the Soferim founded the Rabbinic tradition.

REUBEN

Oldest son of Jacob and Leah. He saved his brother Joseph from death at the hands of his jealous brothers. He is the ancestor of the tribe of Reuben.

REUBEN, TRIBE OF

One of the tribes of Israel. Its territory was east of the Jordan, today the Kingdom of Jordan. The tribe's emblem was a mandrake; its banner was red. The stone representing Reuben in the high priest's breastplate was probably a sardius (ruby).

RIMMONIM

The silver ornaments, with bells, which adorn the top of the Torah scrolls. The Hebrew word "rimmonim" means "pomegranates." In many synagogues the Keter Torah replaces the Rimmonim on special holidays.

RITUAL, SLAUGHTER
see Shehitah

ROCK OF AGES
see Maoz Tzur

ROMANS
Great conquerors of the ancient world, first allies and later enemies of the Hasmonean kings, protectors of the Herodians under whom Judea became a complete vassal of Rome. The Jews repeatedly revolted against Rome. In the Jewish War, Vespasian conquered them in Galilee (66 C.E.). Titus destroyed Jerusalem and the Temple, in 70 C.E. Hadrian's general, Severus, cruelly stamped out Bar Kochba's revolt (132-135) and many Jewish martyrs were put to death. Later Roman rulers were more friendly towards the Jews. Jews migrated to Rome where they became Roman citizens. Under Roman auspices, the first Jews settled as pioneers of trade in parts of Western Europe.

ROSH HASHANAH
(*Beginning of the year*) also called Yom Norah (*Day of Awe*) and Yom Hazikaron (*Day of Remembrance*); the Jewish New Year; first of the High Holy Days of the Jewish year; first of the Ten Days of Penitence. Rosh Hashanah is traditionally regarded as the day of the creation of the world. It is also considered a Day of Judgment, for it is believed that on this day God decides the destinies of all men for the coming year. Though a serious holiday, it is a time for festive joy, because men have an opportunity to repent and begin anew.

(Lev., chap. 23: 23-25; Numbers, chap. 29: 1-6)

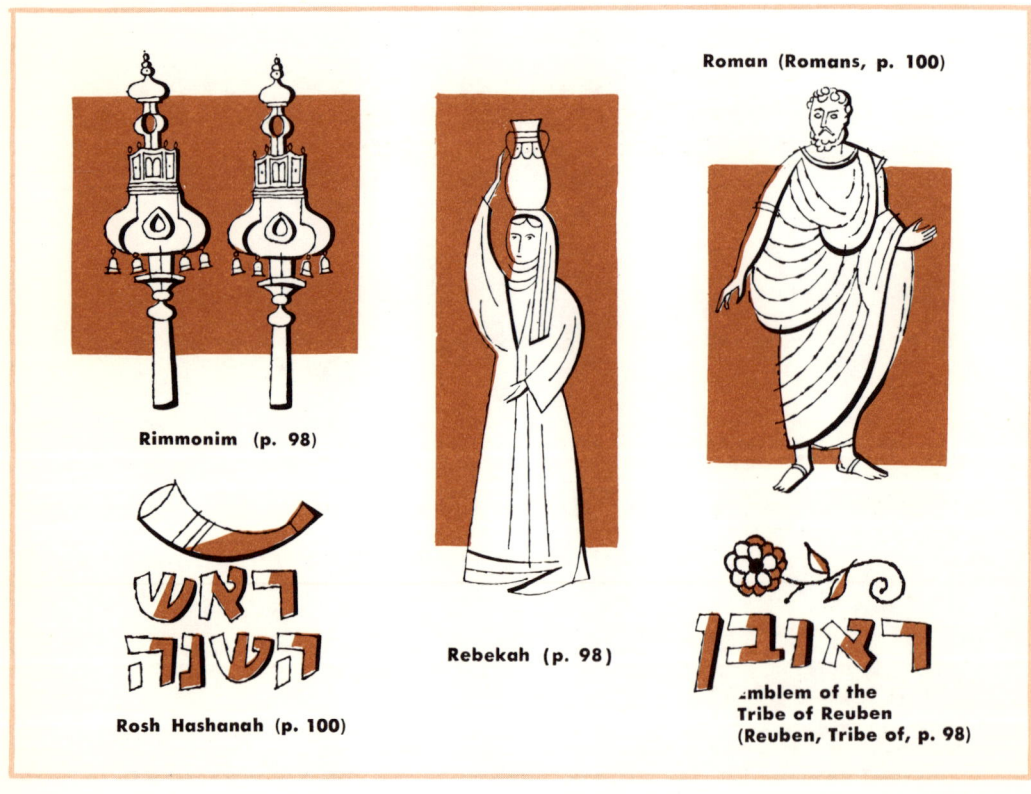

Rimmonim (p. 98)

Rebekah (p. 98)

Rosh Hashanah (p. 100)

Roman (Romans, p. 100)

Emblem of the Tribe of Reuben (Reuben, Tribe of, p. 98)

ROSH HODESH

(*Beginning of the month*) also called New Moon (the new moon determines the beginning of the Jewish month). Rosh Hodesh, in ancient Israel, was a sacred rest day, like the Sabbath; now it is a half-holiday. The Torah is read and special prayers are recited in the synagogue on Rosh Hodesh.

RUTH

The young Moabite widow who faithfully followed Naomi, her Israelite mother-in-law, home to Bethlehem. She married Boaz who saw her work in his field. She was an ancestor of David. Her story is told in the Book of Ruth.

RUTH, BOOK OF

Second of the Five Megillot of the Bible. It tells the story of Ruth, the Moabite great-grandmother of David. The Book of Ruth is read on Shavuot.

SAADIA, BEN JOSEPH

Ga'on at the academy of Sura, Talmudist, scholar, philosopher, writer of commentaries, responsa and liturgical poetry, translator of the Bible into Arabic, and compiler of the first Siddur and the first Hebrew dictionary. Saadia was born in Egypt, 882 C.E., and died in Sura, Babylonia, 942. Saadia gave leadership and strength and a modern interpretation of Judaism to the Jews of his day. He was a man of great personal dignity and integrity.

SABBATH

(*Shabbat*) the weekly holy day of rest, the last day of the week, begins Friday night at sundown and ends at sundown on Saturday evening. A day of rest and a day of sanctification, it is ushered in on Friday night in the home with the lighting of Sabbath candles and the saying of Kiddush. Sabbath services are held in the synagogue on Friday evening and Saturday. At sundown on Saturday, the holy day of Sabbath is ended with the Havdalah ceremony, separating the Sabbath from the workday week.

SABBATH LIGHTS

Candles kindled by the woman of the household as she recites a blessing on Friday evening in honor of the coming of the Sabbath. If there is no woman in the home, the lights may be kindled by a man.

SABBATICAL YEAR

The seventh year during which no agriculture was allowed and all outstanding debts were cancelled. It was observed in this manner in Israel during the time of the Second Temple.
(Leviticus, chaps. 25: 1-7; 20-22)

SABORAIM

Scholars and teachers who lived in Babylonia about the beginning of the 6th century C.E. They supplemented and finished the editing of the Babylonian Talmud, most of which had been collected and written down by Ashi and Rabina.

SADDUCEES

(*Tzeddukim*) Jewish party (sect) during the reign of the Hasmoneans and at the time of the Roman rule of Judea (about the end of the 2nd century B.C.E. through the 1st century C.E.). The Sadducees, party of the and kings. They believed in the strict word of the Torah and rejected Oral

Torah, the teachings of Ezra and the Soferim. The party opposing the Sadducees was the Pharisees.

SAFED

City in Galilee, haven for Sephardic refugees from Spain and Portugal in the 15th and 16th centuries. Safed became a great center of Jewish learning. Joseph Caro, Isaac Ben Luria and other great scholars wrote and taught in Safed.

SALOME ALEXANDRA

Wise and and able queen of Judea (76-67 B.C.E.), wife and successor of the Hasmonean King Alexander Janneaus.

SALT SEA

see Dead Sea

SAMARIA

(*Shomron*) capital of the northern Kingdom of Israel built by King Omri (9th century B.C.E.). Elijah, Amos, Elisha, Hosea and Micah preached in Samaria. The city was destroyed by the Assyrians, after a three year siege; with it fell the Kingdom of Israel, 722 B.C.E.

(Kings I, chap. 16: 23-24; Kings II, chaps. 17: 1-6 and 18: 9-12)

SAMARITANS

According to the Bible, the people imported into Israel by the Assyrians to replace the exiled Israelites after the fall of the Kingdom of Israel in 722 B.C.E. The Samaritans intermarried with the remaining Israelites. When the Judeans returned from Babylonian Exile in 539, they did not accept the Samaritans, believing they had developed a mixed faith. A small group of Samaritans exists today in Nablus, the ancient Shechem. The Samaritans themselves claim that they are descendants of Israelites who remained true to their faith. The ancient Samaritans built their own Temple on Mount Gerizim, which they still regard as a holy site.

(Kings II, chap. 17: 24-41)

SAMSON

Judge and hero of the tribe of Dan, from Zorah, famous for his great strength whose secret source was said to be in his long hair. He was betrayed by Delilah and was taken captive to

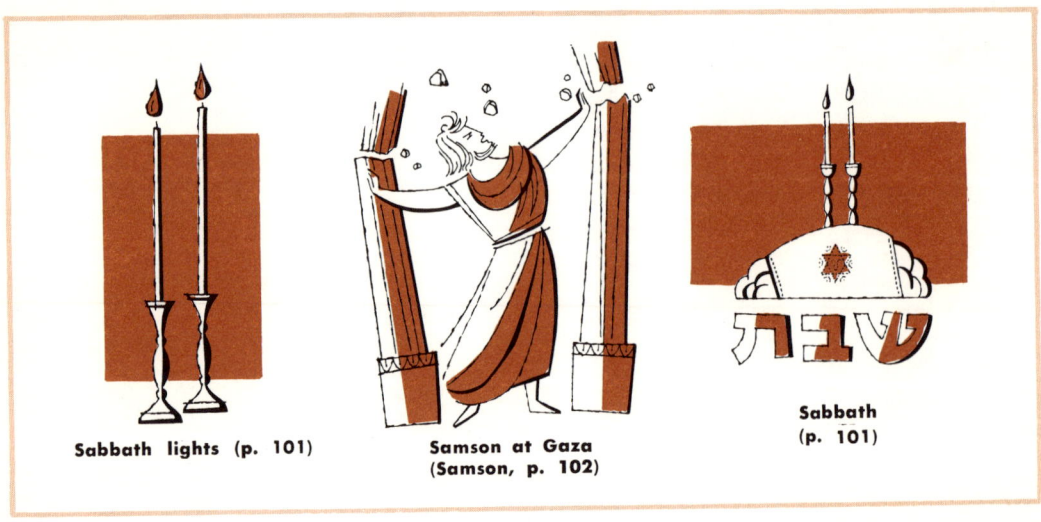

Sabbath lights (p. 101)

Samson at Gaza (Samson, p. 102)

Sabbath (p. 101)

the land of the Philistines. He was blinded and his hair was cut. In a final display of his great strength, he destroyed the Philistines' temple, killing thousands of his tormentors and himself.

(Judges, chaps. 13-16)

SAMUEL

Great judge and prophet (11th century B.C.E.), son of Hannah and Elkanah, student of Eli in Shiloh. After Eli's death and the Philistine victory and capture of the Ark, Samuel judged in Ramah, his home city. He anointed the first two kings in Israel, Saul and David. Two books of the Bible are named after him. Samuel guarded Israel's unity and religious faith during the bitter period of the Philistine's yoke. He is known as one of the great leaders of Israel.

SAMUEL, BAR ABBA

see Mar Samuel

SAMUEL I AND II, BOOKS OF

Third book of the Early Prophets (*Nevi'im Rishonim*) of the Bible. Samuel I records Israel's history from the time of the birth of Samuel to that of the death of Saul. Samuel II records the history of the reign of King David under whom the tribes united and grew into one nation.

SANHEDRIN

(*Assembly*—Hebraicized version of the Greek word "Synedrion"). Trial courts which ruled on matters of Jewish ritual law (Halachah), and on specific civic and criminal cases.

SANHEDRIN, THE GREAT

(The Great Assembly) the highest court and legislative body in the interpretation and formulation of Jewish law in Judea at the time of the Second Temple. It met in halls apparently within the Temple itself, and consisted of 71 men. It was presided over by Zugot *(pairs)*; a Nasi who was head of the legislative sessions, and an Av Bet Din who was head of the legal sessions. After the destruction of the Temple, the Sanhedrin became connected with the (Talmudic) academies.

SARAH

From Ur in the Chaldees, wife of Abraham. She was a beautiful woman of great courage and piety. Late in life she bore Abraham a son, Isaac. She was buried in the Cave of Machpelah. Sarah is the first of the Four Mothers of Israel.

(Genesis, chaps. 12; 18: 1-15; 21: 1-8; 23)

SARAI

Name of Sarah before God's covenant with Abraham.

(Genesis, chap. 17: 15)

SARGON II

Assyrian king, son of Shalmaneser. The city of Samaria fell to him after a three-year siege. He completed the destruction of the Kingdom of Israel and forced its people into captivity.

SAUL

First king of Israel (about 1040 B.C.E.), anointed by Samuel. He united the tribes in the fight against hostile neighbors, especially the strong Philistines. At first he loved young David who cheered him with his harp and songs. Later he turned against David. To avoid being taken alive by the Philistines, Saul had himself killed by one of his own men in the battle of Mount Gilboa.

(Samuel I, chaps. 9-31)

SCHOLAR'S FESTIVAL
see Lag B'omer

SCRIBE
see Sofer

SCROLLS, FIVE
see Megillot, The Five

SEA OF THE PLAIN
see Dead Sea

SEDARIM (OF THE MISHNAH)
(*Divisions, orders*) the six divisions of the Mishnah, each of which is subdivided into Tractates (*massechtot*), chapters (*perakim*) and paragraphs. The six Sedarim are:

1. Zeraim (*Seeds*) : laws concerning agriculture.

2. Moed (*Festival*) : laws regulating the Sabbath, festivals and fast days.

3. Nashim (*Women*) : laws concerning marriage and divorce.

4. Nezikim (*Damages*): civil and criminal laws.

5. Kodashim (*Holy Matters*) : laws concerning the Temple services, sacrifices and Shehitah.

6. Toharot (*Purities*) : laws of ritual purity and cleanliness.

SEDER
The Passover service at home which celebrates the liberation of the Jewish people from Egyptian bondage. In recent times community Seders are held as well as the home Seders. Seder means "order."

SEDER DISH
The platter, often beautifully tooled and designed, which holds the foods eaten during the Seder ceremony. The foods are: (1) a lamb's shank bone, symbolizing the paschal sacrifice; (2) a roasted egg, symbolizing the sacrifice brought to the Temple on festivals; (3) green herbs, usually parsley, symbolizing spring; (4) Haroseth; (5) Maror. A separate dish often holds the Three Matzot, said to stand for the three branches of Israel: Cohen (the priest), Levi (the Levite) and Israel (the people).
see Haroseth
see Maror
see Matzah

SEFER TORAH
see Torah, Sefer

SEFIRAH
Period of Omer, also a time of remembrance of the sufferings of Rabbi Akiba and his students and other scholars under the Roman Emperor Hadrian. According to tradition no weddings or parties are held during the Sefirah period, except on Lag B'omer.

see Lag B' omer

see Omer

Seder Dish (p. 104)

SEIR

Mountainous territory south of the Dead Sea stretching to the Gulf of Aqaba. Esau (Edom) settled there after he lost his birthright. Seir was renamed the Land of Edom. Mount Hor, where Aaron died, is in the region of Seir.

SELIHOT

Prayers of penitence asking for forgiveness of sins. A special group of Selihot prayers are recited in the synagogue during the Ten Days of Penitence (from Rosh Hashanah to Yom Kippur).

SEMIKHAH

(*Support, laying on of hands*) the term used to signify the ordination of a rabbi.

see Ordination

SEMITES

According to the Bible, descendants of Noah's son, Shem. Today people who speak a Semitic language are called Semites (i.e., Arabs who speak Arabic, Jews who speak Hebrew). Semitic is a language classification and not a racial one.

SEPHARDIM

Jews of Spanish or Portuguese descent, a term applied especially to descendants of Jewish exiles and refugees from Spain and Portugal of the 14th and 15th centuries, but now no longer primarily signifying a geographical division of Jewry. Sephardim differ slightly from Ashkenazim in their form of worship and customs but not in their religious beliefs. Sephardic pronunciation of Hebrew differs from the Ashkenazic.

SEPPHORIS

(*Tzipporim*) one of the largest and best fortified cities of Galilee; its capital in Roman times. After the destruction of the Temple, prominent citizens, priests and scholars found refuge there. In the 2nd and 3rd centuries, Sepphoris was a seat of Jewish learning.

see Javneh, Academy of

SEPTUAGINT

The first Greek translation of the Bible. It was prepared by a group of scholars in Alexandria in the 3rd century B.C.E. The Septuagint enabled non-Jews and Jews living in the Greek world who did not know Hebrew to read the Bible. Septuagint is a Greek word meaning "translation of the 70."

SERMON

The sermon which is given during services is a unique part of Judaism that has been adopted by other religious groups. The sermon is usually based on a verse from the Bible which is applied to present times. The popularity and the function of sermons have varied over the centuries.

SETH

Third son of Adam and Eve, born after Abel's murder and Cain's exile to Nod; father of Enosh.

(Genesis, chap. 4:25-26)

SE'UDAH SHELISHIT

Last of the three prescribed meals of Sabbath, held at the end of the day. Se'udah Shelishit is often accompanied by special festivities and singing.

SEXTON
see Shamos

SHABBAT
see Sabbath

SHABBAT BERESHIT
The Sabbath immediately following Simhat Torah on which the yearly cycle of the Torah reading is begun. It is named for the first portion of the Torah, which begins with the word "Bereshit" (*In the beginning*), and which is read on this Sabbath.

SHABBAT HAGADOL
The Sabbath which immediately precedes the holiday of Passover. It is generally accepted that it is called Shabbat Hagadol (*the Great Sabbath*) because the portion from the prophet Malachi read on that day includes the verse: "Behold I will send you Elijah the prophet before the coming of the *great* and terrible day of the Lord" (3:23). On this Sabbath it is customary for the rabbi to deliver a special discourse on the laws and observance of the holiday of Passover.

SHABBAT SHALOM
Greeting on Sabbath, meaning "may you have the Peace of Sabbath."

SHABBAT SHUVAH
The Sabbath that falls between Rosh Hashanah and Yom Kippur. It is called Shabbat Shuvah (*the Sabbath of Return*) because the portion read from the Prophets on that day begins with the words, "Return, O Israel, unto the Lord thy God." On this Sabbath it is customary for the rabbi to deliver a sermon on the laws and principles of teshuvah (*repentance*).

SHADRACH, MESHACH, ABED-NEGO
Daniel's three friends who miraculously survived the fiery furnace into which they were cast by King Nebuchadnezzar of Babylon.
(Daniel, chap. 3)

SHAHARIT
Morning Service, the second of the three daily services (in the Jewish calendar, the day begins at sunset). The prayers of Shaharit are recited early in the morning.

SHALACH MANOT
Exchange of gifts on the day of Purim. Children receive Shalach Manot, usually sweets, on Purim.

SHALLUM
1. King of Israel (about 741 B.C.E.). He assassinated Zechariah, the son of Jeroboam II. Shallum ruled for only one month. He was assassinated and succeeded by Menahem.
(Kings II, chap. 15:8-15)
2. King of Judah, also called Jehoahaz.
(Kings II, chap. 15:8-16)
see Jehoahaz

SHALMANESER V
Assyrian king who led the three-year siege of Samaria, capital of the northern Kingdom of Israel, and took captive its last king, Hoshea. His campaign led to the destruction of the Kingdom of Israel (about 722 B.C.E.).
(Kings II, chap. 17:1-6)

SHALOM
(*Peace*) the traditional Jewish salutation used in greetings and farewells.

SHALOM ALECHEM
1. Traditional greeting which means "peace be unto you."
2. Beautiful Sabbath song, sung especially on the eve of Sabbath.

SHALOSH REGALIM
(*The Three Festivals of Pilgrimage*) Passover, Shavuot and Sukkot. In ancient times these festivals were observed by making pilgrimages to the Temple or other places of worship.
(Deut., chap. 16:1-17)

SHAMGAR
Hero and third Judge of Israel, son of Anath. He defeated the Philistines.
(Judges, chap. 3:31)

SHAMIR
According to Jewish legend, the miraculous little worm who could split the greatest stones, used by King Solomon in building the Temple. Iron tools could not be used in building this sacred house because they were symbols of war. The legends of the Shamir are many and very colorful.

SHAMMAI
Brilliant scholar and teacher of the 1st century B.C.E., Av Bet Din, colleague and opponent of the great Hillel. Hillel and Shammai were the last of the five Zugot *(pairs)* of the Great Sanhedrin. Shammai kept to the letter of the law and was strict, while Hillel was more lenient and gentle. Some of their brilliant discussions and those of their schools were recorded in the Mishnah.

see Zugot

SHAMOS
1. (*Sexton*) also called Shamosh, the man in charge of the synagogue building.
2. The "helper" candle used to light the other eight candles of the Hanukkah Menorah.

SHAVUOT
(*The Feast of Weeks*) one of the three ancient harvest and pilgrimage festivals, a holiday that celebrates the first harvest and also commemorates the giving of the Ten Commandments at Mount Sinai. It is observed seven weeks after Passover. In some congregations, confirmation exercises are held during this festival.
(Lev., chap., 23: 15-21; Deut., chap. 16: 9-12)

SHEBA, QUEEN OF
The wise and wealthy queen who came to visit King Solomon because the fame of his wisdom and splendor had reached her in her faraway Arabian kingdom. She declared that what she had seen for herself far exceeded the reports she had heard.
(Kings I, chap. 10: 1-13)

SHECHEM
Ancient city northeast of Samaria, seat of Jeroboam, first king of the northern Kingdom of Israel. Many Biblical events took place in Shechem. Joseph is said to be buried there. Joshua assembled the tribes at Shechem to speak to them before his death. It was one of the Cities of Refuge.

see Cities of Refuge

SHEHITAH
(*Ritual slaughter*) the specific rules stated by the rabbis for the manner and method of sanitary and humane slaughtering of animals for food. The

three main requirements for kosher slaughtering are the employment of a Shohet, the use of a proper knife, and the administering of a painless cut.

SHEKEL
Weight in very ancient times with which metal was weighed, in later Biblical times the coin and money-value of Israel and Judah. The yearly tax to help maintain the Temple was half a shekel.

SHEKHINAH
see Hasidism

SHEM
Oldest of the three sons of Noah. According to Biblical tradition, he is the ancestor of the Semitic peoples.
(Genesis, chap. 10:21)

SHEMA
(*Hear*) the first word of the prayer which forms the central concept of the Jewish religion: "Hear O Israel: the Lord our God, the Lord is One."
(Deut., chap. 6:4)

see Keriat Shema

SHEMINI ATZERET
(*Eighth Day of Solemn Assembly*) eighth day of the Sukkot holiday. Technically a separate holiday, it is observed in practice as the concluding day of Sukkot. Special prayers for rain are recited on this day.
(Lev., chap. 23:36)

SHEMONEH ESREH
The Eighteen Benedictions recited at each of the daily services, the most important prayers of petition in the Jewish liturgy, and the core of religious service. The Shemoneh Esreh is recited in silent devotion, while the worshippers stand, facing east. Shemoneh Esreh means "eighteen." This prayer is also referred to as the "Amidah."

see Amidah

SHEMOT
see Exodus, Book of

SHESHBAZZAR
Prince of the House of David, sometimes identified as Zerubbabel. He led the first Jews back to Judea at the time of King Cyrus.
(Ezra, chap. 1:8-11)

SHEVARIM
see Shofar

SHEVAT
Fifth month in the Jewish calendar.
see Months, Jewish

SHIELD OF DAVID
(*Magen David*) a six-pointed star consisting of two interlaced triangles, in modern times the generally accepted symbol of Judaism. Its history is ancient and goes back to Biblical times. The Magen David occupies the center of the flag of Israel.

SHILOH
Town in Ephraim where Joshua established the first sanctuary of the Ark. After the death of Eli, Shiloh was destroyed by the Philistines.
(Joshua, chap. 18:1; Samuel I, chap. 4)

SHIR HAMAALOT
1. (*Song of Ascents, Song of Steps*) refers to 15 Psalms from the Biblical Book of Psalms (120-134). The Shir

Hamaalot were probably sung on the Three Pilgrimage Festivals and by the Judeans returning from Babylonian Exile. At the time of the Second Temple, the Levites sang these Psalms on fifteen designated steps of the Temple.

2. Refers specifically to Psalm 126 sung at Grace after Meals on the Sabbath and festivals.

SHIR HASHIRIM
see Song of Songs

SHIVAH
(*Seven*) seven-day mourning period. Mourners refrain from work and sit Shivah at home during this week. Among some congregations the period of mourning has been shortened to three days.

SHIVAH ASAR BETAMMUZ
(*Fast Day of the Seventeenth of Tammuz*) fast day observed in commemoration of the first break in the wall of Jerusalem by the Babylonians in the year 586 B.C.E.

SHOFAR
A ram's horn, used in ancient times to signal an alarm or to assemble the people. The Shofar is sounded on Rosh Hashanah and Yom Kippur. Its stirring notes are understood as an announcement of the New Year and as a divine summons to repentance and improvement. The three notes sounded on the Shofar are called Tekiah (*blowing*), Teruah (*alarm*) and Shevarim (*tremolo*).

(Numbers, chap. 10:1-10; Lev., chap. 23:23-25)

SHOFETIM
see Judges

see Judges, Book of

SHOHET
Slaughterer of animals and fowls in accordance with Jewish ritual. The Shohet must be an observant Jew who has thoroughly studied the laws of Shehitah and who has received a written license from a rabbi, certifying that he has been examined and approved.

Shofar (p. 109)

Ancient Judean silver coin (Shekel, p. 108)

Shavuot (p. 107)

Magen David (Shield of David, p. 108)

SHOMRON
see Samaria

SHUL
Yiddish word for synagogue.

SHULAMIT
(*Peaceful One*) the shepherdess whose loveliness is extolled in the Song of Songs.

SHULHAN ARUKH
Famous code of Jewish law, first published about 1565 in Safed, Palestine. It was written by Joseph Caro (born in Toledo, Spain, 1488, died in Safed, 1575). The Shulhan Arukh (based on the Arba Turim by Jacob ben Asher), which deals with ritual and legal matters, is simply arranged so that it can be used by everyone. Shulhan Arukh means "the set table"—the laws are arranged so that everyone can help himself to them, as he would to food at a prepared table.

SHUSHAN
(Or Susa) capital of ancient Persia, scene of the events described in the Book of Esther.

SHUSHAN PURIM
A half-holiday which occurs the day after Purim. It celebrates the festivities which took place in the city of Shushan, the scene of the Purim story, after the Jews were saved.

SIDDUR
Prayer book, a volume containing the prayers for daily and Sabbath worship, arranged in a given order. The Siddur also contains some prayers for the holidays. Saadia compiled the first Siddur in the 10th century.

SIDRAH
see Parashah

SIFRE EMET
(*Book of Truth*) the three poetical books, the first part of Ketubim (the third division of the Bible), containing Psalms, Proverbs and Job.

See Ketubim

SIMEON
Second son of Jacob and Leah, ancestor of the tribe of Simeon.

see Simeon, Tribe of

SIMEON BAR YOHAI
Tannaitic scholar and teacher of the 2nd century C.E., student of Akiba. Simeon had to flee from the Romans, and for 13 years hid in a cave. Simeon was a mystic. Legend has it that he was the author of the Zohar (great work of Cabala which appeared in Spain in the 13th century). On Lag B'omer, the day of Simeon's death, pilgrims visit his grave at Merom, near Safed.

SIMEON BEN LAKHISH
Great Amora, scholar and teacher one of the founders of the Palestinian Talmud, colleague and friend of Johanan Bar Nappaha. Many legends exist about Simeon. He is said to have been a circus animal-trainer and perhaps a leader of a band of thieves before he became a great rabbi. Simeon's brilliant discussions with Johanan Bar Nappaha are recorded in the Talmud.

SIMEON, TRIBE OF
One of the tribes of Israel. Its territory was south of the tribe of Judah and included Beer-sheba, the south-

ernmost point in Israel. Its emblem was the city of Shechem; its banner was green. The stone representing Simeon in the high priest's breastplate was probably a topaz.

SIMHAT TORAH

The holiday which occurs the day after Shemini Atzeret. It celebrates the end of a year's reading from the Torah, and the beginning of the year's new reading, which starts with the first chapter of Genesis (*Bereshit*). Simhat Torah means "rejoicing over the Torah."

SIMON

Son of Mattathias, head of Judea and high priest; brother of Judah Maccabee.

SIN

see Zin

SINAI, MOUNT

The mountain in the Sinai Desert where Moses received the Ten Commandments.

(Exodus, chaps. 19-20)

SIRACH

Book of the Apocrypha, also called Ecclesiasticus, containing wise sayings and rules for conduct.

SISERA

General of the Canaanite King Jabin, defeated by Deborah and Barak in a battle at Mount Tabor. He fled and was killed by a Kenite woman, Jael, in whose tent he sought refuge.

(Judges, chap. 4)

SIVAN

Ninth month in the Jewish calendar.

see Months, Jewish

SKULLCAP

Headpiece. The custom of covering the head, though not based on Biblical or Talmudic law, is observed by the majority of Jews. It developed in medieval times. The skullcap is called "Kippah" in Hebrew and "Yarmulka" in Yiddish.

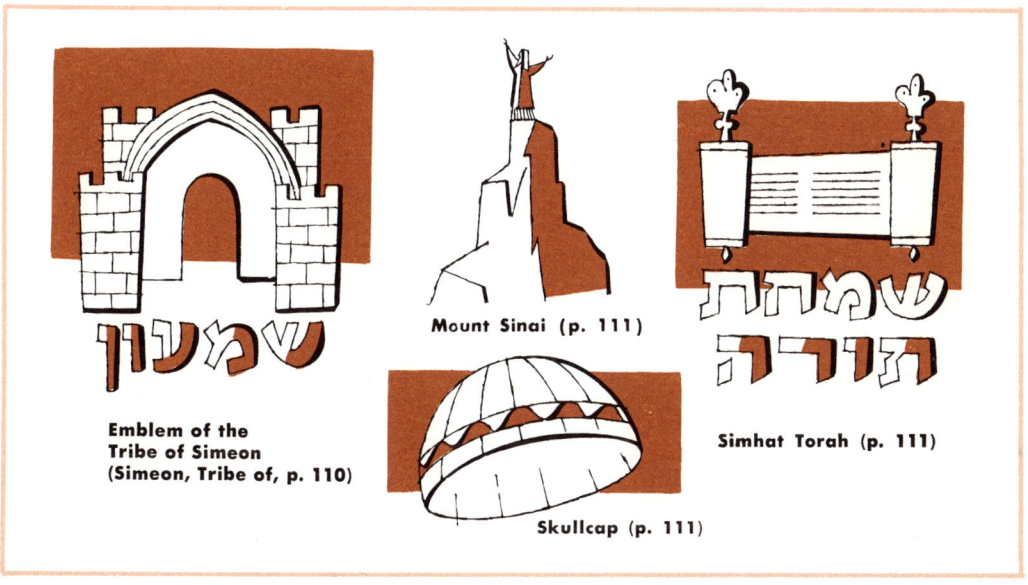

Emblem of the Tribe of Simeon
(Simeon, Tribe of, p. 110)

Mount Sinai (p. 111)

Skullcap (p. 111)

Simhat Torah (p. 111)

SLAUGHTER, RITUAL
see Shehitah

SODOM AND GOMORRAH
The two most important of the five Cities of the Plain; destroyed for their wickedness and inhospitality. Only the household of Lot, who lived in Sodom, was saved—except for his wife who was turned into a pillar of salt because she looked back at the destroyed cities. The ruins of Sodom and Gomorrah lie at the bottom of the Dead Sea.

(Genesis, chaps. 18-19)

SOFER
A scribe, the man who writes by hand the sacred Torah scrolls in accordance with prescribed rules. He is expected to be a very pious man.

SOFERIM
The scholars from the time of Ezra to that of the Zugot who studied and interpreted the Torah (5th to 3rd centuries B.C.E.). Some of their teachings, with those of the Zugot, came down to the Tannaim and are recorded in the Mishnah.

SOLOMON
Third king of Israel (about 977-937 B.C.E.), son of David and Bath-sheba, builder of the beautiful First Temple. During his peaceful reign, he made Jerusalem a great city and developed Israel's trade and commerce with Egypt, Phoenicia, Arabia and even India, through the construction of a fleet and the mining of copper. His wise judgments and sayings brought him fame. He is considered the author of three Biblical books: Song of Songs, Proverbs and Ecclesiastes.

(Kings I, chaps. 1-11)

SONG OF SONGS
(*Shir Hashirim*) first of the Five Megillot of the Bible. This beautiful poem is considered to represent the love between God and Israel. It is ascribed to King Solomon. The poem is read in the synagogue on Passover.

SPICEBOX
(*Besamim* box) used in the Havdalah ceremony marking the end of the Sabbath and the festivals in the traditional synagogue and home. A

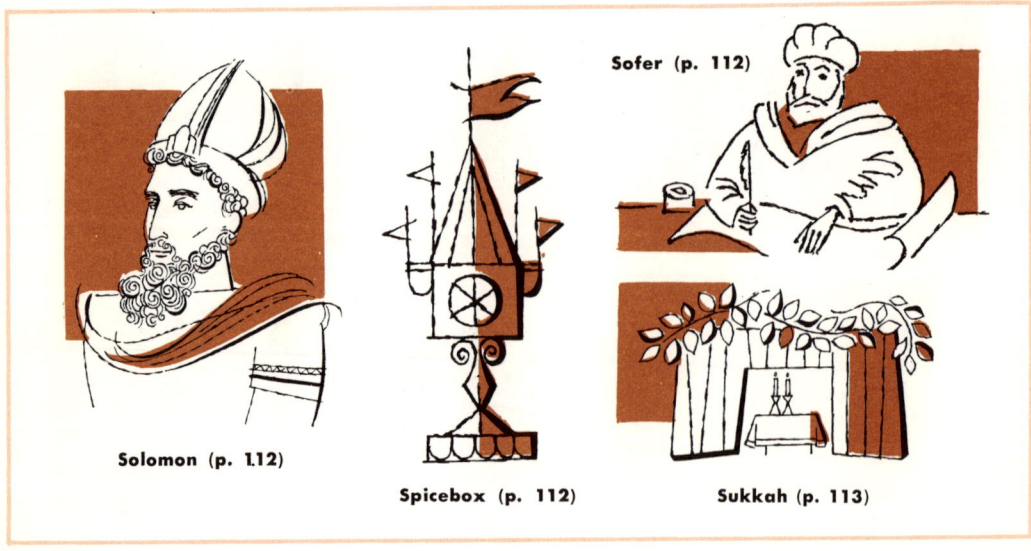

Solomon (p. 112)

Sofer (p. 112)

Spicebox (p. 112)

Sukkah (p. 113)

112

prayer is made over the spices which are inhaled as a remembrance of the beauty of the Sabbath (or festival).

STAR OF DAVID
see Shield of David

SUKKAH
A booth or hut made of branches and decorated with fruits and flowers, used during the holiday of Sukkot. These temporary huts are a reminder of the Israelites' wanderings in the wilderness, and serve as a place to thank God for His many blessings.

(Leviticus, chap. 23: 42-43)

SUKKOT
(*Feast of Tabernacles*) one of the three ancient harvest and pilgrimage festivals, the thanksgiving and harvest holiday which occurs five days after Yom Kippur. It was the custom during this festival to dwell in Sukkot (*booths*).

(Lev., chap. 23: 33-43)

SUKKOT, FOUR PLANTS OF
Ethrog (*citron*), Lulav (*palm*), Hadas (*myrtle*) and Aravah (*willow*); four plants used by the Jewish people since ancient times when they carried them in the joyous processions of the Pilgrimage festival of Sukkot to the Temple in Jerusalem. Lulav, Aravah and Hadas, bound together, are held with the Ethrog. These plants symbolize that God is everywhere and that, like the four plants, all Jews are bound together in brotherhood.

(Lev., chap. 23: 40)

SURA
One of the three most famous Babylonian Talmudic academies, founded in the 3rd century, a foremost seat of Jewish learning. Saadia was Ga'on of the Sura academy in the 10th century.

SYNAGOGUE
Greek word meaning "assembly" or "congregation," first used by the Jews of Egypt in the 3rd century B.C.E. to describe their houses of worship. Today most Orthodox and Conservative congregations use this word; Reform congregations usually use the Latin word "temple." The Yiddish word for synagogue is "shul."

SYRIA
Originally ancient Aram, conquered and annexed to Assyria in the 8th century B.C.E. Syria was conquered successively by the Babylonians, the Persians, and Alexander the Great

Sukkot, Four Plants of (p. 113)

סוכות
Sukkot (p. 113)

Modern Synagogue
(Synagogue, p. 113)

113

(333 B.C.E.). After Alexander's death, the Seleucide kings ruled over Syria from Antioch, their capital. Judea then was their vassal. The Maccabees led the Judean revolt against the Syrian King, Antiochus IV. The modern republic of Syria, northern neighbor of the State of Israel, was established in 1942.

TAANIT BEHORIM

(*Fast of the First-Born*) a fast day on the 14th of Nisan, on the eve of Passover, observed by first-born sons, in remembrance of the sparing of Israel's first-born, when the angel of death, who struck the unfortunate first-born sons of the Egyptians, "passed over" the houses of the Israelites.

(Exodus, chap. 12: 21-27)

TAANIT ESTHER

(*The Fast of Esther*) a fast day commemorating the fast of the Jews of Persia, led by Esther and Mordecai, who were threatened with death by Haman. Taanit Esther occurs on the 13th of Adar, the day before Purim.

TABERNACLE

The portable sanctuary used by the Israelites during their wanderings in the wilderness. The Ark of the Covenant was kept in its inner shrine, the Holy of Holies. The Tabernacle was dedicated by Moses. It was also called the "Tent of the Meeting."

See Ohel Moed

TABLES OF THE LAW

The two stone tablets upon which were engraved the Ten Commandments, also called "Tablets of the Law," or "Tablets of the Covenant" (*Luchot Ha B'rit*).

TABOR, MOUNT

Northeast of the Emek Jezreel, near the Kishon River, in ancient times a beautifully wooded mountain, often mentioned as a symbol of God's strength. Near Mount Tabor, Deborah and Barak defeated the army of Sisera and King Jabin.

TALLIT

A fringed prayer shawl, traditionally worn by men and boys over 13 when reciting prayers. Some worshippers kiss the Tallit before putting it on, as a token of reverence, and make a benediction. It is not worn by most Reform Jews.

TALMUD

Great book of post-Biblical writings on Jewish law and lore based on Oral Torah which in turn is based on the Torah. The Talmud consists of the Mishnah and the Gemara. There are two different versions of the Talmud, the Palestinian and the Babylonian; each is based on the same Mishnah but has its own Gemara.

TALMUD, BABYLONIAN

One of the two versions of the Talmud. It consists of the Mishnah, the Toseftah (supplement to the Mishnah) and the Babylonian Gemara. It was edited by Rabina and Ashi and was completed by the Saboraim in the beginning of the 6th century C.E. It is longer and more complete than the Palestinian Talmud and is more frequently used.

TALMUD, PALESTINIAN

Consists of the Mishnah and the Palestinian Gemara, completed by the Palestinian Amoraim by the middle of the 4th century C.E. It is older and shorter than the Babylonian Talmud. Though not compiled in Jerusalem, its Hebrew name is "Talmud Yerushalmi."

TALMUD TORAH

An afternoon school for the "teaching of the Torah," attended by students after their elementary school session.

TAMMUZ

Tenth month in the Jewish calendar.

see Months, Jewish

TANAKH

The Bible in its entirety; an abbreviation of the names of the three major divisions of the Bible:

1. Torah (Five Books of Moses);
2. Nevi'im (the Prophetic Books);
3. Ketubim (Writings).

see Bible

TANNAIM

(*Teachers* in Aramaic) teachers and scholars whose discussions and commentaries on Jewish law are recorded in the Mishnah. The period of the Tannaim (1st to 3rd centuries C.E.) started with the death of Hillel and ended with the death of Judah Hanasi.

TARGUM

(*Translation* in Aramaic) refers specifically to Aramaic translations of Hebrew texts, usually parts of the Bible, written at the time when Aramaic was the everyday language of most Jews. The best known early Targum of the Torah is Targum Onkelos, written approximately in the 2nd and 3rd centuries C.E. The later Targum Yerushalmi (written approximately from the 4th to the 7th centuries C.E.) includes Midrashic passages.

TAS

see Breastplate

TEFILLAH

(*Prayer*) originally described only prayers of petition or thanksgiving, applied specifically to Shemoneh Esreh. Today the word is used to describe any prayer.

TEFILLIN

Small leather boxes which contain four handwritten sections of the Torah and to which leather straps are attached. Traditionally, men and boys over 13 place these on the head and left arm during daily morning prayers except on Sabbaths and holidays. The tradition of putting on of Tefillin (*phylacteries*) is derived from the Biblical commandment, "And thou shalt bind them for a sign upon thy hand, and they shall be for frontlets between thine eyes."

(Deut., chap 6: 8)

TEHILLIM

see Psalms, Book of

TEKIAH

see Shofar

TEMPLE, FIRST AND SECOND

The beautiful First Temple was built by King Solomon in Jerusalem. It was the spiritual center of Israel for about 400 years, until it was destroyed by Nebuchadnezzar in 586 B.C.E. The Second Temple was rebuilt by the returning Babylonian exiles in 520 B.C.E. It was in existence until 70 C.E., when it was leveled to the ground by the Romans. Since then the restoration of the Temple has been one of the cherished hopes of the Jews.

**(Kings I, chaps 6-8;
Kings II, chap. 25;
Ezra, chaps. 5-6)**

THE TALMUDIC AGE

SOFERIM (*scribes*)
Fifth to Third centuries B.C.E.

The generations of scholars and teachers who carried on the work of EZRA.

ZUGOT (*pairs*)
Second century B.C.E. until about 10 C.E.

The two leaders of the great Sanhedrin who carried on the teachings and interpretations of the Torah after the period of the Soferim. HILLEL and SHAMMAI were the last and most brilliant of the Zugot.

TANNAIM (*teachers*)
First and Second centuries C.E.

The scholars and teachers whose works are recorded in the Mishnah.

- 41   GAMALIEL I, Nasi and last president of the Great Sanhedrin.
- 70   JOHANAN BEN ZAKKAI, founder of the academy of Javneh.
- 80   GAMALIEL II, Nasi and head of the Sanhedrin and of the academy at Javneh.
- 130   RABBI AKIBA.
- 138   RABBI MEIR and SIMEON BAR YOHAI.
- 165–200   JUDAH HANASI (Judah I), Nasi, head of the Sanhedrin and the academy, compiler of the Mishnah.

AMORAIM (*speakers*)
Third to Sixth centuries C.E.
(about 200-499)

The scholars and teachers whose work is recorded in the Gemara.

- 210   GAMALIEL III, son of Judah Hanasi, head of the academy and of the Sanhedrin.
- 219   *ABBA AREKHA (RAV) and MAR SAMUEL founded the Babylonian Talmud.
- 225   JOHANAN BAR NAPPAHA and SIMEON BEN LAKHISH.
- 259   HILLEL II, Nasi and head of the academy and of the Sanhedrin, introduced the fixed calendar.
- 370   Completion of the Palestinian Talmud.
- 425   GAMALIEL IV, last Nasi. End of Patriarchate.
- 354–427   *ASHI and
- 499   RABINA, compiled the Babylonian Talmud.

SABORAIM (*reasoners*)
500 until 530 C.E.

The scholars and teachers who completed the editing of the Babylonian Talmud. Until the time of the Gaonate great Babylonian scholars bore the title of SABORA.

FOR LATER EXPOUNDERS OF TORAH AND TALMUD SEE:

Gaon, Saadia, Maimonides, Rashi, Tosafists

also see *Codes of Jewish Law*

This chart refers to only a few of the many Talmudic scholars. Babylonian scholars are marked with an asterisk*.

TEN COMMANDMENTS

The ten rules for conduct toward God and man that form the basis of Jewish religious and moral law. According to the Bible, these laws were given by God to Moses at Mount Sinai, and engraved upon the two Tablets of the Law.

1. I am the Lord thy God who brought thee out of the land of Egypt, out of the house of bondage.
2. Thou shalt have no other gods before me.
3. Thou shalt not take the name of the Lord thy God in vain.
4. Remember the Sabbath day to keep it holy.
5. Honour thy father and mother.
6. Thou shalt not murder.
7. Thou shalt not commit adultery.
8. Thou shalt not steal.
9. Thou shalt not bear false witness.
10. Thou shalt not covet.

(Exodus, chap. 20: 1-17;
Deut., chap. 5: 6-18)

TEN DAYS OF PENITENCE

The days from Rosh Hashanah to Yom Kippur, inclusive. These days are devoted to repentance. Penitential prayers (*Selihot*) are said during this time. These days are also called Days of Awe (*Yamim Noraim*).

TEN PLAGUES

see Plagues, The Ten

TERAH

Father of Abraham, Nahor and Haran. Terah and his family left their home in Ur of the Chaldees and moved to the city of Haran, where they settled. Abraham left his family to live in Canaan, the land God had promised him.

(Genesis, chap. 11: 24-32)

TEREFAH

(*Forbidden*) foods that are forbidden according to Jewish dietary laws. Not all Jews accept these laws as binding.

see Dietary Laws

see Kosher

TERUAH

see Shofar

TESHUVOT

see Responsa

TEVET

Fourth month in the Jewish calendar.

see Months, Jewish

THIRTEEN ARTICLES OF FAITH

see Maimonides

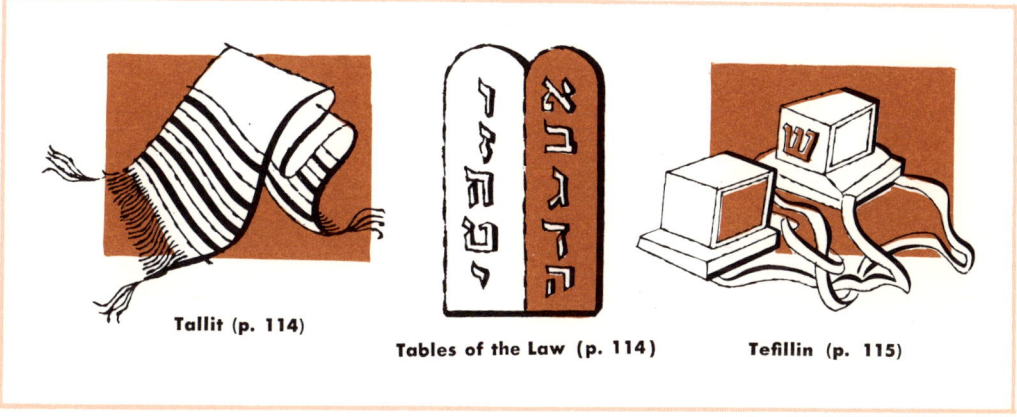

Tallit (p. 114)   Tables of the Law (p. 114)   Tefillin (p. 115)

THREE FESTIVALS
see Shalosh Regalim

TIBERIAS
City on the Sea of Galilee founded by King Antipas and named in honor of the Roman Emperor Tiberius. In the Jewish War, the fortress Tiberias was a center of Jewish revolt. In the 3rd century it became the seat of the Patriarchate *(Nasi)* and the home of an important Talmudic academy.

TISHAH B'AV
(The Ninth Day of the Month of Av) a day of fasting and prayer in commemoration of the destruction of the First and the Second Temples in Jerusalem and the fall of the fortress of Betar at the end of Bar Kochba's revolt.

TISHRI
First month in the Jewish calendar.
see Months, Jewish

TOBIT, BOOK OF
Book of the Apocrypha. It relates the story of Tobit, the pious Israelite who compassionately buried the Israelites slain in Assyrian Exile.

TOHAROT
see Sedarim

TOLA
A judge of Israel, of the tribe of Issachar. Tola judged 23 years.
(Judges 10:1-2)

TOMBSTONES
The custom of placing monuments on graves dates back at least to the time of Jacob who is said to have erected a pillar to mark the tomb of Rachel. Tombstones are usually erected eleven months after the time of burial. A special service is held at the unveiling.

TORAH
The Five Books of Moses, the foundation of the Jewish tradition and faith; Torah also means learning, teaching, guidance and law. The Torah is the great spiritual inheritance of Israel. Torah, worship and benevolence are, according to the rabbis, the three pillars that uphold Judaism; but Torah is the strongest pillar on which the others are built.

TORAH, ORAL
see Oral Torah.

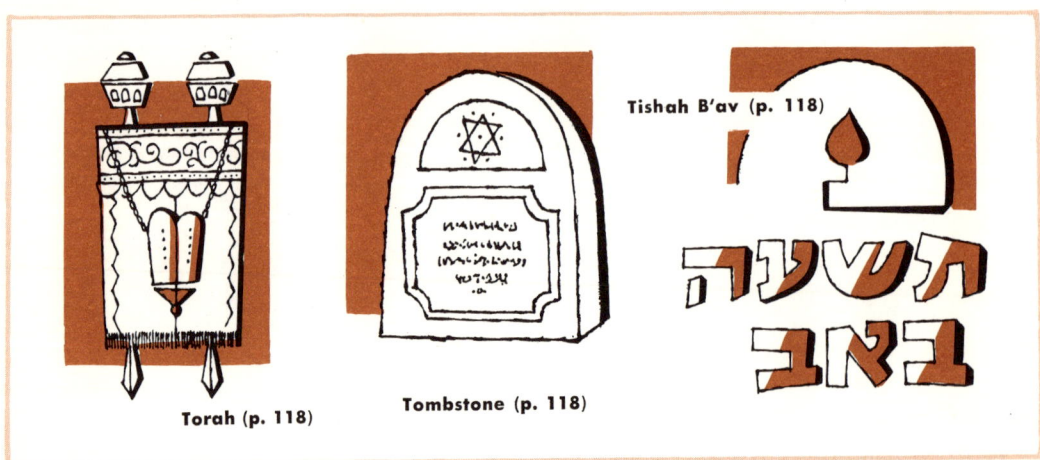

Torah (p. 118)

Tombstone (p. 118)

Tishah B'av (p. 118)

TORAH, READING OF

Portions (*parshiyot*) of the Torah are read in the synagogue on every Sabbath of the year and on holidays and special days, such as Rosh Hodesh. The portions which are read on Sabbath are so arranged that over the year the entire Pentateuch (the Torah) is completed. On holidays and special days, selected portions chosen for their relevance to that particular day are read. Originally, each person called up to the reading of the Torah was expected to read a section by himself, but it has now become the custom for especially trained people to read the portion for those given an Aliyah.

TORAH, SEFER

The Scroll of the Torah, handwritten on special parchment by the sofer. The Sefer Torah is a large scroll, mounted on two rollers. Each synagogue usually has several scrolls, from which portions of the Torah are read at their prescribed times. If a Sefer Torah cannot be used any more, it is buried or stored in a Genizah.

TOSAFOT

(*Additions*) commentaries on selected passages of the Talmud. They were written by the Talmudic scholars (Tosafists) of France and Western Germany in the 12th and 13th centuries. In editions of the Talmud, Tosafot are printed on the outer side of a page, while Rashi's continuous commentaries are printed on the inner side of the page. One of the important Tosafists was Rabbenu Tam (Jacob ben Meir) grandson of Rashi.

TOSEFTAH

Additional commentaries on the Mishnah, edited by the Amoraim of Babylonia.

TOWER OF BABEL

The high tower built by the descendants of Noah in the land of Shinar (Babylonia). In Genesis it is told that God punished the builders for trying to reach the heavens by making each of them speak a different language and scattering them all over the world.

(Genesis, chap. 11: 1-9)

TROPP

The ancient musical signs used to indicate to the reader of the Torah, the Haftarah and other parts of the Bible, the melodies in which they are to be chanted.

TU BISHVAT

see Hamishah Asar Bishvat

TURIM

1. The four rows (*Arba Turim*) of the twelve precious stones representing the twelve tribes of Israel in the high priest's breastplate.

2. A code of Jewish law named after the Turim, compiled by Jacob Ben Asher (also called Baal Turim, born in Germany, 1269, died in Spain, 1340). The Turim is a code of law designed for everyday use. It is arranged in four divisions and is also called Tur. It was used by Caro as the basis for the Shulhan Arukh.

TWELVE PROPHETS

see Prophets, Twelve

TWELVE TRIBES

The divisions of the nation of Israel during the time of the Judges and the early kings. The Twelve Tribes were descendants of the 12 sons of Jacob-Israel. Each tribe received a portion of land when the Israelites entered Canaan after their Exodus from Egypt. The priestly tribe of Levi did not take a portion, but the division into 12 sections was maintained, since the portion of Joseph was divided between his two sons, Ephraim and Manasseh. The tribes slowly lost their distinct identities when Israel became a more consolidated nation.

THE TRIBES OF ISRAEL

Name	Emblem	Banner	Jewel
JUDAH	lion	sky-blue	emerald
ISSACHAR	donkey	black, the sun and the moon	sapphire
ZEBULUN	ship	white	diamond
REUBEN	mandrake	red	sardius (ruby)
SIMEON	City of Shechem	green	topaz
GAD	encampment	gray	agate
EPHRAIM	bullock	jet-black	onyx
MANASSEH	unicorn	jet-black	onyx
BENJAMIN	wolf	many-colored	jasper
DAN	serpent	deep blue	ligure (emerald)
NAPHTALI	deer	wine-color	amethyst
ASHER	woman and an olive tree	pearl-color	beryl
LEVI	urim and tummim	white, red and black	carbuncle

EMBLEMS OF THE TRIBES OF ISRAEL

Judah   Issachar   Zebulun   Reuben   Simeon   Gad

Ephraim Manasseh   Benjamin   Dan   Naphtali   Asher   Levi

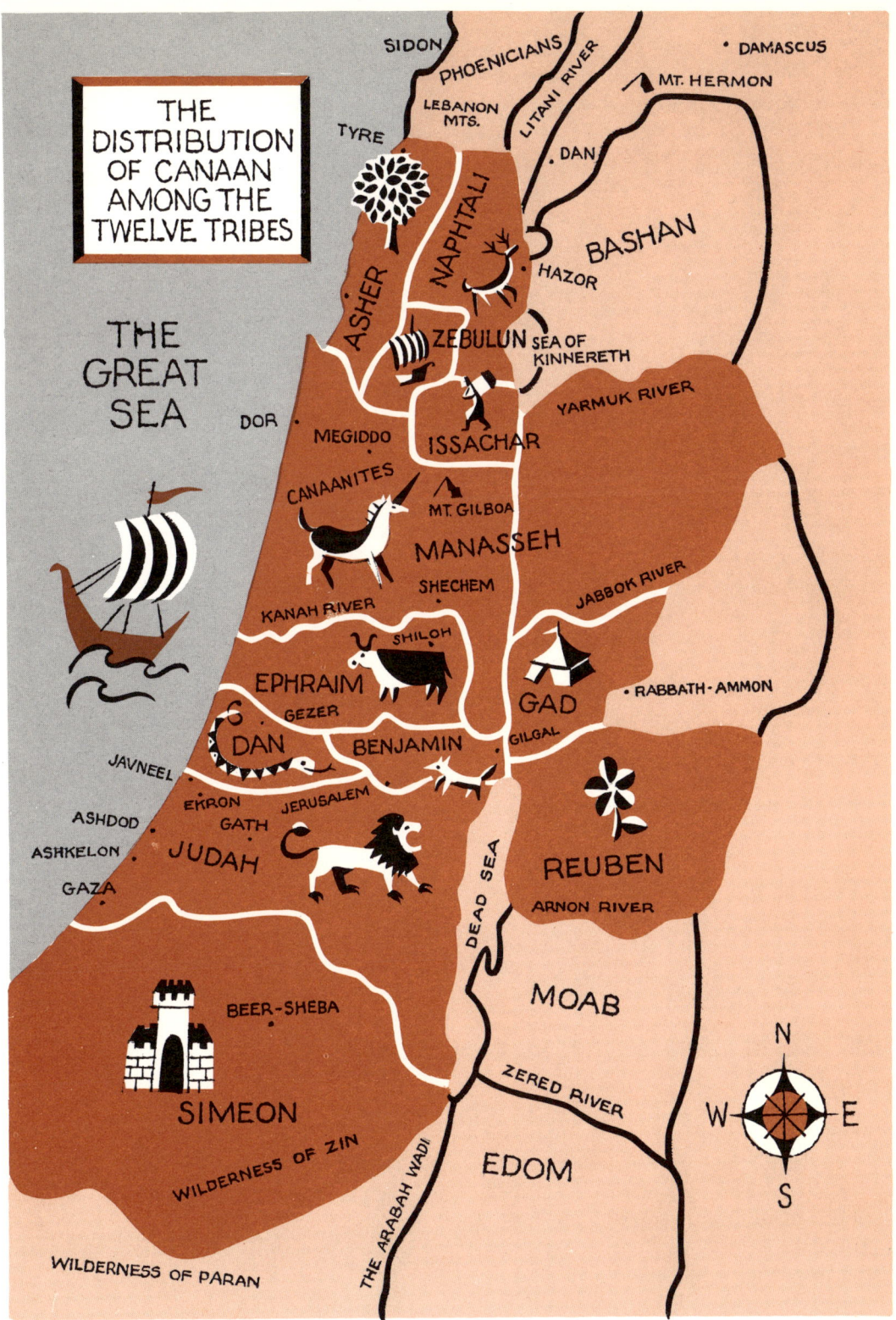

TYRE

Royal city of the kings of ancient Phoenicia; great port and trade city of antiquity on the coast of the Mediterranean, now called Sur. King Hiram, ally of David and Solomon, lived there. The prized city was taken by the Assyrians, Babylonians, Syrians and by Alexander the Great. Phoenicians of Tyre are said to have founded Carthage, the great rival of Rome.

TZITZIT

The fringes on the prayer shawl (*Tallit*) and the Arba Kanfot.
(Numbers, chap. 15:37-41)
see Fringes

TZOM GEDALIAH

(*The Fast of Gedaliah*) a day of fasting and mourning commemorating the assassination of Gedaliah, the governor of Judea.

see Gedaliah

URIAH

Brave officer of King David's army, husband of Bath-sheba whom David later married. Uriah was sent into a raging battle where he died.
(Samuel II, chap. 11)

URIEL

Angel and messenger of God.

URIM and TUMMIM

(*Light and Truth*) probably two sacred objects the high priest carried under the Breastplate of Judgment. Some scholars today believe that the Urim and Tummim were really identical with the four rows of the twelve precious stones in the breastplate, representing the Twelve Tribes of Israel. The high priest wore the Urim and Tummim upon his heart when he stood before God in prayer and in search of advice and judgment. The Latin form of Urim and Tummim (*lux et veritas*) is the motto of Yale University.
(Exodus, chap. 28: 1-30)

UR OF THE CHALDEES

Ancient city on the Euphrates, the birthplace of Abraham.

USHA

City in Galilee, seat of the Sanhedrin (2nd century C.E.) and of an academy of Tannaim.

UZZIAH

Also called Azariah; son of Amaziah; father of Jotham; tenth king of Judah at the time of Jeroboam II of Israel. During his long reign (about 767-737 B.C.E.) he upheld the religion of the One God. He fortified Jerusalem, strengthened the army and held in check his country's foes. Judah flourished under the reign of Uzziah.
(Kings II, chap. 15:1-7; Chron. II, chap. 26)

VASHTI

Queen of Persia, wife of King Ahasuerus. She refused to appear before his guests and was cast out of the royal household. Esther succeeded her as Queen of Persia.

VAYIKRA

see Leviticus, Book of

VEADAR

see Adar Sheni

WAILING WALL

(*Kotel Maaravi*, "western wall") last remnant of the Temple on the Temple Mount in Jerusalem. For centuries Jews made pilgrimages to pray at this sacred spot. Today it is in the part of Jerusalem that belongs to Jordan, and is inaccessible to Jews.

WEDDING

see Hatunah

WILLOW

see Aravah

see Hoshanot

WISDOM OF SOLOMON

Book of the Apocrypha consisting of discourses and wise sayings.

XERXES

see Ahasuerus

YAD

(*Hand*) a pointer usually made of precious metal. It is used by the reader as a guide in pointing out the text to be read from the Torah.

YAD HAZAKAH

see Mishneh Torah.

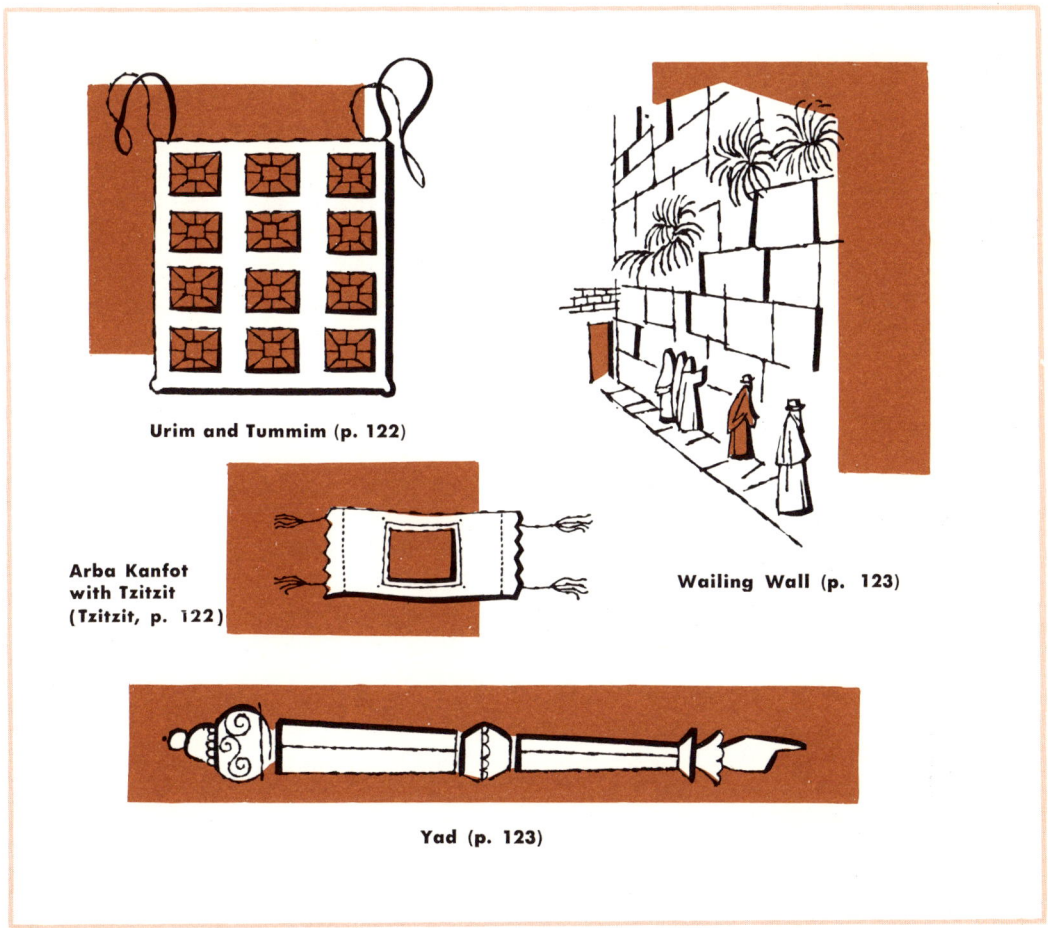

Urim and Tummim (p. 122)

Arba Kanfot with Tzitzit (Tzitzit, p. 122)

Wailing Wall (p. 123)

Yad (p. 123)

YAHRZEIT

The anniversary of the day of the death of a parent or other close relative. It is observed by the lighting of a Yahrzeit candle or light in the home, and the recital of Kaddish in the synagogue.

YAMIM NORAIM

see Rosh Hashanah

see Ten Days of Penitence

see Yom Kippur

YAM SUF

see Red Sea

YARHINAAH

see Mar Samuel

YARMULKA

see Skullcap

YEAR, JEWISH

see Months, Jewish

YEHUDI

see Jew

YERUSHALMI

see Talmud, Palestinian

YESHIVA

(*Academy*) originally a school of higher Jewish learning for which students were eligible after completing Talmud Torah or Heder. In modern times the term is often applied to Jewish elementary all-day schools in which students receive a secular and a Jewish education. New York's Yeshiva University is a prominent school of higher Jewish learning in the United States.

YETZIAT MITZRAIM

see Exodus

YEMENITE JEWS

Jews of the Arabic kingdom of Yemen; first settled there after the destruction of the first Temple. After the rise of Islam they suffered for centuries from discriminatory laws and poverty. Today only few Jews live in Yemen, since 46,000 Jews were evacuated to Israel in 1949 and 1950 in "Operation Magic Carpet." Their fine carpet weavers and silversmiths and their songs and dances contribute to the new culture of Israel.

YIDDISH

Everyday language of many Ashkenazic Jews all over the world, developed in medieval times by the German Jews who had migrated to Eastern Europe. Yiddish was based on medieval German and on Hebrew. Later, Yiddish incorporated some words from other languages. Many religious books, literary works, folk songs and tales are written in the Yiddish language. Yiddish newspapers appear in many parts of the world.

YISKOR

(*May He Remember*) refers to the memorial services for the departed recited in the synagogue on Yom Kippur and on the last day of Passover and Shavuot and on Shemini Atzeret.

YOM HAZIKARON

see Rosh Hashanah

YOM KIPPUR

(*Day of Atonement*) the holiest day of the Jewish religious year, the last day of the Ten Days of Penitence. It is a fast day during which the Jew seeks forgiveness for his sins and reconciliation with God and his fellowmen. Yom Kippur, the climax of the Ten Days of Penitence, is also called Yom Norah (*Day of Awe*).

(Lev., chap. 23: 26-32)

ZADDIK

A completely righteous man. A Zaddik is just to his fellowmen and observes God's commandments. The leaders of the Hasidic movement often are called by the title Zaddik. According to Jewish legend, there are always thirty-six Zaddikim unrecognized and ignorant of their righteousness, to whose piety the world owes its existence.

ZADOK

With Abiathar, priest at the time of David. He helped David bring the Ark to Jerusalem. Zadok supported Solomon as David's successor and was made sole high priest under Solomon. He was the ancestor of many high priests.

(Kings I, chaps. 1: 8 and 32-39; chap. 2: 35)

ZEBOIIM

One of the Cities of the Plain.

see Cities of the Plain

ZEBULUN

Tenth son of Jacob, sixth son of Leah, ancestor of the tribe of Zebulun.

ZEBULUN, TRIBE OF

One of the tribes of Israel. Its territory was in the rich and fertile northern region of Israel. Zebulun became part of the northern Kingdom of Israel. The tribe's emblem was a ship; its banner was white. The stone representing Zebulun in the high priest's breastplate was probably a diamond.

ZECHARIAH

1. Eleventh of the Books of Twelve (Minor) Prophets of the Bible. The prophet Zechariah was a contemporary of Zerubbabel, Haggai and the high priest Joshua. He helped in the building of the Second Temple. His writings contain visions and prophecies.

2. Fourteenth king of Israel, son of Jeroboam II. After a rule of six months, Zechariah was assassinated and succeeded by Shallum (about 741 B.C.E.).

(Kings II, chap. 15: 8-12)

Yahrzeit candle (Yahrzeit, p. 124)

Emblem of the Tribe of Zebulun (Zebulun, Tribe of, p. 125)

Yom Kippur (p. 124)

ZEDAKAH

(*Charity*) righteousness, justice. The Jewish belief in Zedakah is based not simply on pity for the needy but also on the principle of justice and the belief that all men are brothers.

ZEDEKIAH

Also called Mattaniah, twentieth and last king of Judah (about 597-586 B.C.E., before the Babylonian Exile), son of King Josiah, renamed and appointed king by Nebuchadnezzar. Ignoring the warnings of the prophet Jeremiah, he revolted against mighty Babylonia and was defeated. Jerusalem and the beautiful Temple of Solomon were destroyed. Zedekiah was blinded and imprisoned, and, with his people, carried into Babylonian captivity.

(Kings II, chap. 24: 17-chap. 25:7)

ZEPHANIAH

Ninth of the Books of Twelve (Minor) Prophets of the Bible. The prophet Zephaniah preached in the early years of the reign of King Josiah of Judah. He spoke bitterly against the corrupt conditions before Josiah's great reforms.

ZERAIM

see Sedarim

ZERUBBABEL

Governor of Judea, grandson of King Jehoiachin of Judah. At the time of King Cyrus of Persia, this prince of the House of David led the first Jews back from Babylon. With the help of the high priest Joshua and the prophets Haggai and Zechariah, Zerubbabel started to build the Second Temple.

(Ezra, chaps. 1 and 5)

see Sheshbazzar

ZIKLAG

Philistine city near Gaza where David found refuge from King Saul. The Philistine king, Achish, gave Ziklag to David, who stayed there with his followers until the death of King Saul.

(Samuel I, chap. 27)

ZILPAH

Maid of Leah and secondary wife of Jacob. She was the mother of Gad and Asher, ancestors of tribes of Israel.

(Genesis, chap. 30: 9-13)

ZIMRI

Captain of the guard who assassinated King Elah and reigned as King of Israel for seven days (about 889 B.C.E.). When Omri attempted to dethrone him, Zimri burned the palace and killed himself in the flames.

(Kings I, chap. 16: 9-20)

ZIN

One of the four wildernesses of the Sinai Peninsula through which the Israelites wandered to Canaan, southwest of the Dead Sea region.

ZIONISM

The movement, founded in the second half of the 19th century, which aimed at the return of the Jewish people to the land of Israel as their national homeland, and at the creation of a political Jewish community there. Since the founding of the new State of Israel in 1948, the Zionist movement has worked for the growth and strengthening of the new State.

ZION, MOUNT

Mountain in Jerusalem, originally the site of the Jebusite fortress captured by David. David built his castle on Zion and Solomon built the Temple there. The Second Temple was also built on Mount Zion. Later, Zion became a symbol for Jerusalem and Israel. As it is said: "For out of Zion shall go forth the Torah, and the word of the Lord from Jerusalem." At the time of Abraham, Mount Zion was known as Mount Moriah.

see Moriah, Mount

ZIPPORAH

Shepherdess, daughter of Jethro the Kenite priest of Midian. She became the wife of Moses when he found refuge with Jethro in Midian, after slaying Pharaoh's taskmaster. Zipporah bore Moses two sons, Gershom and Eliezer.

(Exodus, chaps. 2: 21-22; 18: 1-4)

ZOAR

The only one of the five Cities of the Plain, in the Dead Sea region, saved from destruction. It was saved for Lot's sake who found refuge there. Zoar was a town in Moab.

(Genesis, chap. 19: 18-22)

see Cities of the Plain

ZOHAR

(*Bright light*) major book of the Cabala, appeared first in Spain in the 13th century. Its author was probably Moses Ben Shemtov de Leon, though it has been ascribed to Rabbi Simeon Bar Yohai, famous Palestinian mystic scholar of the 2nd century C.E. The Zohar contains the central teachings of Jewish mysticism.

ZUGOT

(*Pairs*) the two scholarly religious leaders who presided over the Great Sanhedrin; the Nasi (who was head of the Sanhedrin and presided over its legislative sessions) and the Av Bet Din (who presided over its legal sessions). Five successive Zugot carried on the traditions of study and interpretation of the Torah from the period of the Soferim to that of the Tannaim. The last and best known of the Zugot were Hillel and Shammai. Some of their teachings came down through the Tannaim and were recorded in the Mishnah. After Hillel, the office of Av Bet Din was either dissolved or held by the Nasi himself.

see Sanhedrin, The Great